Breaking Into THE REO BUSINESS

How I Went From Bankruptcy
To $7.2 Million in 7 Years
While Making Friends

Tony Alvarez

Montana Publishing Company
Lancaster, CA

Breaking into the REO Business: How I Went from Bankruptcy to $7.2 Million in 7 Years While Making Friends
by Tony Alvarez

Library of Congress Control Number: 2010913369

ISBN: 978-1-45373-4-902

Second Edition, 2010

Published in the United States of America

Published by:
Montana Publishing Company
P.O. Box 9072
Lancaster, CA 93539

Cover and typesetting by Susie Ward, www.SGWDesign.com

Warning – Disclaimer

This book is designed to provide information on real estate investing. It is sold with the understanding that the publisher and author are not engaged in rendering legal, accounting or other professional services. If legal or other expert assistance is required, the services of a competent professional should be sought.

It is not the purpose of this book to reprint all the information that is otherwise available to real estate investors, but instead to complement, amplify and supplement other texts. You are urged to read all the available material, learn as much as possible about real estate investing and tailor the information to your individual needs. For more information, see the many resources available in the Appendix.

Real estate investing is not a get-rich-quick scheme. Anyone who decides to invest in real estate must expect to put a lot of time and effort into it. For many people, real estate investing is more lucrative than investing their money in the stock market, mutual funds, Treasury Bonds and the like, and many have built solid growing rewarding real estate investing businesses.

Every effort has been made to make this book as complete and as accurate as possible. However, there may be mistakes, both typographical and in content. Therefore, this text should be used only as a general guide and not as the ultimate source of real estate investing. Furthermore, this book contains information on real estate investing that is current only up to the printing date and/or the real estate market conditions at the time of the book's conception.

The purpose of this book is to educate and entertain. The author and publisher shall have neither liability nor responsibility to any person or entity with respect to any loss or damage caused, or alleged to have been caused, directly or indirectly, by the information contained in this book.

If you do not wish to be bound by the above, you may return this book to the author or publisher for a full refund.

Read This First!

Hi. This is Tony Alvarez. I want to take a moment to explain how this book was put together for your convenience.

First of all, this entire book was based on my personal experience going from bankruptcy to making millions which I presented on behalf of The Norris Group for a group of professional real estate investors at "The Millionaire Maker Series" seminar in Southern California.

This book is divided into 3 sections.

Section 1: The Book

Breaking Into The REO Business: How I Went From Bankruptcy to $7.2 Million in 7 Years While Making Friends

This is the whole story, and perfect for the few of you who love to read, and actually read the books and do the exercises from all the courses that you buy.

Section 2: The Outline

The Path of Least Resistance

This is the actual outline that was in my hand when I gave the presentation. For those of you more like me who don't like to read, but who want to go straight to the meat of the material, this section is for you.

Section 3: 14 Distinctions that Gave Me the Edge

This is for people ***exactly*** like me! The lazy and incompetent. This section includes the most important distinctions I've identified as responsible for the financial success I've achieved.

Now here's my suggestion.

READ ALL THREE SECTIONS in whatever order you like.

Why?

Because doing this will help you increase your retention of the most important parts of this material quickly. That way, this doesn't become another one of those books you bought, put in your bookcase and never read. Just choose one section and get going.

And Heaven help you if you EVER call me or ask me a question (if the answer can be found in the pages of this book) because all you're ever going to get from me is a dial tone.

By the way, what you do with what you learn from this book is entirely up to you, and any result or lack thereof is your sole responsibility.

The bottom line is this:

This book is filled with my own personal opinions, my point of view, and my suggestions based on my life experiences. You may or may not agree with them, and of course, that is your option.

However, that is as far as they go.

I promise nothing. Nor do I guarantee you anything; not results, your happiness, your financial success, or that you will be loved by the masses.

Just like me or any other person who has achieved any level of success, you are on your own. How you perceive what you read on these pages or hear me say (or how you interpret this information) is entirely in your control and your responsibility.

Best of Luck!

Love,

Uncle Tony

This book is dedicated to my grandson,

Lucas Montana Alvarez,

who fills my heart with love and hope for the future.

You are the best of everything I have ever known.

Tony and Lucas Alvarez

This is a love story. Not your typical love story, but a love story just the same. If you read carefully, you will see that love abounds on each page; sometimes obvious, sometimes not. It's no secret, I love what I do, but I sincerely love each and every agent I've ever worked with on a deal. For without their hard work, dedication and friendship, I would still be chasing my dream. So to all the agents, past, present and future, thank you for helping me change my life. You will forever be in my heart.

Big Hug,
Uncle Tony

About the Author

Tony Alvarez has been a successful real estate investor and certified general appraiser in Southern California area since 1981.

More importantly, Tony made a fortune buying and selling properties while working with professional real estate agents that specialize in selling REO (real estate owned) foreclosed lender-owned properties. He did it all in seven years and in one of the lowest priced most depressed Southern California real estate markets, the Antelope Valley.

Tony has purchased, rehabbed, rented and sold hundreds of properties from vacant land to condos, single family residences, apartments and commercial properties.

Tony started his real estate career working as a staff appraiser for Great Western and Glendale Federal Bank and is approved by hundreds of lenders and insurance companies, as well as government agencies. He has worked with Fannie Mae, Freddie Mac, FHA, FDIC and the RTC (Resolution Trust Corp.) He has an in-depth knowledge of the inner workings of lenders and their real estate owned (REO) lender-owned property departments.

Tony's knowledge of real estate, appraisal, finance, and investing is vast and varied. He brings a unique perspective to the real estate investment community.

Tony is a sought-after speaker and instructor and has previously spoken at The Norris Group's Multi-Millionaire Maker series in 2005 and 2006, as well as other real estate investment clubs and top real estate offices throughout Southern California. Although Tony made over $7.2 million in the last downturn, he still manages his own rental property business from the same "ugly little office" he's been working out of for years. Tony also teaches courses and classes, as well as coaches and mentors new up-and-coming real estate investors on how to get the edge making millions buying, selling, renting and managing distressed properties in this crazy unpredictable real estate market.

A NOTE FROM MY FRIEND BRUCE NORRIS

FOREWORD

Tony Alvarez is one of those rare people who just puts a smile on people's faces by just being himself. Two stories tell everything you need to know about the character of Tony Alvarez.

Tony was speaking at a Riverside investment club meeting and sharing some of the deals he was putting together. Someone near the front kept on saying something to the effect, "Man, you really robbed those people blind on that one!"

This misdirected individual spurred Tony to do something I had never seen before or since. Just to prove that the people who sold him their houses were treated fairly, Tony shows up at each of the houses with a cameraman.

You can tell the people are surprised because some of them are chewing dinner or picking some chicken out of their teeth! But to a person, everyone was delighted to see "Uncle" Tony! Tony, it seems, makes friends of even the people who sell him properties at a discount. Tony asked them a series of questions about why they had sold their house to him for less than it was worth.

The answers they gave were absolutely classic and their responses, if understood and replicated, can make you wealthy. What's funny is they don't really know why they sold Tony their house... but I do. Their answers were tangible, but what moved them to action was intangible. (I'll get back to this in a moment).

The other story is about a man who owned a home Tony met one day {after considerable persistence on Tony's part}. It seems that this man had given up on life. Tony finally coaxed the man to open his door and saw someone akin to Rip Van Winkle with three-inch nails. Life had so beaten down this homeowner, he had hidden inside his house for years. Tony took the time to listen to the man and decided for him that it was time to get back his life.

Tony goes to the store and buys the man everything he needs to get back on his feet. In essence, he saved the man's life. In that act of kindness lies the strength of Tony Alvarez as a person and a property buyer. Imbedded in his nature is first and foremost a love for people. People feel it, and they trust Tony. Don't take that sentence lightly... people don't trust people they just meet, but they trust Tony.

Tony didn't care about buying the guy's property until he cared for the person. He bought the other people's houses for exactly the same reason and following the same sequence... love/trust/cooperation. If this sounds like a sales technique to you, you are missing the point.

If you decide to have Tony Alvarez teach you, be prepared to change who you are. Be prepared to change how you see people. Be prepared to change how you do business. Be prepared to look across the table at whomever it is (a realtor/property owner/fellow investor) and think first of how you can be of genuine service to them.

Tony Alvarez and Bruce Norris

There are three world-renowned trainers who have clearly understood what Tony understands. In Zig Ziglar's classic book *See You at the Top*, Ziglar states, "You can get everything in life you want if you help enough other people get what they want."

Ben Gay III called the concept becoming a “sales infiltrator” in his great sales book, *Closers #2.* A sales infiltrator has in essence “earned” the right to make decisions for others because of your willingness to act only in their best interest.

In Stephen Covey’s *The 8th Habit,* he talks about the concept of the speed of trust.

“But when there’s high trust, communication is easy and instantaneous. Mistakes hardly matter, because people trust you: “Don’t worry about it. I understand.” No technology ever devised can do that. There is nothing as fast as the speed of trust. When trust is present, mistakes are forgiven and forgotten.

Tony Alvarez is successful because first and foremost he loves people. People pick that up, and in return they trust him. Then Tony looks at their situation and helps them make a decision. If it sounds easy, it isn’t. Is it worth your time to learn? The concepts made Tony a very wealthy man, and that allows him to spend time doing what he’s most passionate about…. making a difference in people’s lives!

Tony, thank you, my friend, for the privilege of allowing me to write this foreword to what I know will open a new world of opportunity for those who are willing to listen to what you have to say.

Sincerely,

Bruce Norris

THANK YOU ALL FOR HELPING

Acknowledgments

This is an extremely difficult task to say the least, no matter how hard I try to remember everyone I'm absolutely sure I will screw this up. So here goes…

First, I want to thank you and all other Americans for allowing my family (and all immigrants who have been as fortunate) to come to this wonderful country, for without this freedom that we are so blessed to enjoy, I would not be able to write these words you are presently reading.

I'm eternally grateful to all the folks that have had anything to do with supporting me throughout this arduous process, starting with my staff.

To my loyal, hardworking assistant, Sabrina, who's been with me for many years, who has never missed one of my boring speaking engagements and has always upheld the company motto, "Make Tony Look Good." Thank you for always trying so hard to fulfill my often unrealistic demands. You've never let me down. Words cannot express what you mean to me. Thank you, well, for EVERYTHING! Without you, I'd have to close up shop and move back to Cuba.

To our new friend Susie Ward, without whose help, knowledge, patience and expertise this book would have never been completed. You made the process seamless and actually pleasurable. I look forward to the next one.

To my brothers and sister for their love & love & love and close friendship. Through the toughest of times, you all added in some way to who I have become. We will always be connected.

A big hug and juicy kiss (on the cheek of course) to my good friend Bruce Norris who had the foresight, wisdom and intelligence to see something in me I did not see myself when he courageously offered to have me speak for the first time in my life before his audience at the first Millionaire Maker Seminar Series. Thanks for your faith in me, and for the $3 million your 10 words helped me make – you never stop giving!

A special thanks to other professional investors and good friends like Bill Tan, Mike Cantu, Mick Blackwell, Rick Solis, Andrea Esplin, Jack Fullerton, Nick Manfredi, Shawn Watkins, Angel Bronsgeest, Steve and Robyn Love, Ward Hanigan, Miles Lipovich (who took it upon himself to write "We Love You Tony" on the chalk board behind me the first time I ever spoke publicly), and many more of you who are presently trapped inside my ADD ridden mind. You all have helped to shape my opinions, decisions and bottom line based on your advice over the years.

To all of my real estate appraisal buddies, headed by Bill Swift and Bob Blanchard, who helped me with their wisdom and friendship through the '80s, '90s and now this third wave.

To the professional REO agents who have put up with my nonsense, became good friends, and made me filthy rich throughout the years; including my very best friend Don Anderson who is mostly responsible for making me wealthy and forever changing my family's financial future. A big hug and thanks; you are a good and trusted friend. And let's not forget J.C. Boucher, Charla Abbott and many, many others that I've come to know and love.

Also, I'd like to thank Dave Del Dotto and the rest of those guys that taught real estate back in the '70s (even though I'm not sure if they ever bought a single house) for keeping me company late at night with the very first infomercials I ever saw, giving me hope that I could, in fact, one day become a successful real estate investor. Dave now owns a wonderful vineyard with absolutely fantastic wine in Napa (www.DelDottoVinyards.com). Thanks, Dave, for helping me get into the real estate game.

A big hug to my dad, who taught me the value of commitment and hard work. Thanks, Pop. I love you.

To my loving mother, who has always been the most positive influence in my life, who taught me the value of building long-term relationships by learning to love and care for other people first. Te quiero mucho, Mom.

A heartwarming thanks to Catherine Ann Riley, the first woman after my mother to ever believe in me and my crazy schemes. I can never repay you for the love, loyalty, commitment and support you so kindly bestowed on me and my son. You are one of my most trusted, closest friends and deepest confidant. Thank you. I love you dearly.

To my close friend Guy Finley, who has dedicated his life to helping us all find the value and truth of our lives, and showing me how to bring forth the best of myself.

And to the love of my life, Danna, the person I share my life with, without whose love, patience, understanding, help and unwavering support (as well as English and typing skills) I would have never been able to complete this task. Thank you for bringing true love to me at this stage in my life. Your love, kindness and never-ending thoughtfulness are a consistent reminder of the best in all of us. I love you.

I love you all.

Tony Alvarez and Danna Prosser

A SPECIAL MESSAGE FROM TONY ALVAREZ

Before You Get Started

I'd like to start by telling you a little bit about my past. I think this is important because as you get further into this book and into the practical application of the things I've done to succeed in the real estate industry, I believe you will see threads of my past carefully interwoven into who I ultimately became in business, and who I am today. This, I have come to understand, was vital to my success and might also be to yours.

In addition, and more importantly, I want to thank you for purchasing my book. I am sincerely grateful; I really mean that. Thank you very much for believing in me, for that is exactly what you do when you purchase a book. What you're really saying is, "I believe in you, Tony, and I think it's worth my money and my time to buy and read what you wrote." This is probably the highest compliment that you can pay anyone who has written anything, but in my case, it's huge!

A Little History

You see, I really wasn't meant to write anything. I wasn't really even meant to succeed at anything. What I mean is the odds were definitely stacked against me, and in all honesty, I think given a chance I would have even bet against myself.

Let me start by explaining that I was not born in the United States. I was born in Havana, Cuba in 1955 to wonderful, hardworking and loving parents just before the Castro revolution took hold.

Although my father had a very cushy job working as a clerk of courts in the same courthouse where my grandfather, his father, worked as a judge, he and my mother (who worked as a school teacher) decided to leave everything they knew — their family, friends, jobs, homes, all of their possessions — to bring me and my brothers to the United States so we would be free from Communism.

We migrated to America in 1960 when I was 5 years old. This is a sacrifice my mother and father made for us that I will never be able to repay. Just like I will never be able to repay this great country for allowing us to come here and enjoy the freedoms most Americans take for granted daily. Please forgive me if what I just wrote made you feel uncomfortable; that was not my intent. I just wanted you to know I never forget how grateful I must always be to all Americans who gave my family the opportunity to come here and participate in the greatest gift America offers, Freedom! The freedom to choose to work hard towards any achievement we desire, or to choose to simply do nothing.

I Never Had a Chance

Now as for the odds being stacked against me, look at this list: First I was diagnosed with ADD caused by early childhood trauma to the skull. That simply means I fell out of my crib when I was 2 and landed head first on a tile floor. I actually stopped breathing, but my dad rushed over and saved me by picking me up and, while holding me with his hands firmly placed under my arms, shook me until I started breathing again. Yup, that's right. It's a miracle I'm not in a coma still! Anyway, I spent most of my younger years as a severe asthmatic and introvert, meaning I did not speak to anyone, ever, for anything. Nobody knows why or exactly when I decided to come out of my psychological, self-imposed cave. My mother says one day I just started talking, and have never shut up since.

I'm No Genius

My whole life I have been a terrible student, and my favorite subject has always been history. I think it's because history is like storytelling and about real people; everything else usually bored me to death. I can't spell or punctuate two sentences correctly. English is my worst subject, only to be outdone by math; without a calculator, I'm toast! In the eighth grade when all the other students were preparing to pick a high school that would prepare them for college, the nun in charge of my class (we attended Catholic school) called my mother into school for an urgent conference. As I stood there between them, Sister Marie proceeded to inform my mother that I really was not college material, and it would be better if she placed me in a vocational school so I could learn a trade; a suggestion my mother took as if from God himself and promptly found and signed me up at Lawrence Regional Vocational Technical High School. I was always amazed at how they got that whole name to fit on the side of the school bus. I ended up dropping out of high school in the last month of my senior year, which was a huge disappointment to my mother (sorry, Mom) who always insisted I was brilliant and who has always been, and is still to this day, the most positive influence in my entire life.

Rina & Antonio Alvarez - Mom & Dad

Coming to America

Like most Cubans, we landed in Miami penniless not knowing one word of English and with no contacts or connections of any kind.

My parents got jobs doing anything they could. My father washed dishes, and my mother became a maid. But the allure of the textile mills in New England with their higher paying jobs soon had us all on a Greyhound bus to Lawrence, Massachusetts. And that's where we spent the better part of our youth until migrating to California. From my father, I learned to keep my head down and work harder than anyone else, and from my mother I quickly learned the art of relationship building. Those are two distinctly different sides of the same success-building coin, which I would later come to understand as absolutely essential to not only achieving, but holding onto any level of long-term success in this life.

It Was Never Easy

I suppose I make it sound easy, but it wasn't. We were, in fact, the first Spanish speaking family in that wonderful mill town, and we paid the price any new immigrant pays for being different than the status quo. But you won't hear any complaints here. We loved every minute of our life and would not change one thing. Some of the best friends I have had and still love, I met in that town.

Yes, we had tough times, but in all honesty, they pale in comparison to one day of battle any American soldier has experienced while defending the freedoms which were so graciously bestowed upon my family and me from the moment we arrived in this great country.

We all learned a lot from those early years, it's all part of the fiber and foundation of the people we've become. We survived and grew strong in the awareness that not only was anything possible, but we having made it to America while others not as fortunate had not, left us with a sense of responsibility to do with our lives anything and everything possible. We were constantly reminded that we stood on the shoulders of those who came before us, and we must do better and never forget to extend a hand to all that cross our paths in solemn gratitude for all we have been given.

Who Needs the Details?

I will not go into the details of all the experiences that shaped my family's lives, as I am saving that for a book I am presently finishing for my mother titled ***Never Look Back***. Suffice it to say, that we made it thanks to my parents' courage, persistence and determination. It should come as no great surprise that my first two heroes and mentors are and will always be my mother and father.

Starting Out

I started my career as an in-house real estate appraiser working for Great Western Bank and then for Glendale Federal Bank in Southern California. During the recession of the 1990s, I worked as a contract appraiser for RTC (Resolution Trust Corp.) I have spent most of my adult working life within the real estate industry either as a real estate appraiser, investor, instructor, teacher, mentor, coach, or all of the above. I have been a certified general appraiser, residential property rehabber, property manager, broker, and California state-approved real estate course provider. I have appraised, owned, sold, rented or invested in thousands of properties, including everything from vacant land to 100,000 square-foot commercial shopping centers. During my real estate business life, I have experienced many ups and downs, even bankruptcy. There are few mistakes I have not perfected. I have made many decisions, some good and some not so good, but overall I have weathered many storms and came out okay; actually better than okay.

I've Been There Before

I understand where you are because my butt has warmed many a seat at seminars, just like you're probably doing today. It was not too long ago that I was broke and trying to find a way to get a dream to believe in, one that would inspire me to keep going.

I found it in the real estate business. I gave myself over to it, studied hard for the first time in my life, worked even harder, without restriction, and persisted until I was rewarded. And rewarded I have been.

I sincerely hope that something in these pages inspires and helps to deliver you to the financial freedom I have been so fortunate to be blessed with, and that you achieve the level of financial peace of mind you deserve.

Best wishes,

Uncle Tony

Contents

All our dreams can come true, if we have

the courage to pursue them.

- Walt Disney

WITHIN THE PAGES OF THIS BOOK

Introduction

Within these pages, I have presented to you the very best of what I have learned while working in the real estate industry. What I believe are the true principles, distinctions, and decisions I made that took me from broke financially and in spirit to a place in my life where my bank balance is always above six figures and where waking up every day brings with it a wonderful underlying sense of freedom I can only hope you have already achieved.

Please be aware that since I started investing in real estate in 1980 through today, most of my income has come from buying, fixing, selling or renting small, inexpensive residential properties nobody wanted, while working specifically with REO real estate brokers and agents. For many years, other investors would hear of my success and seek me out for lunch and advice on how to duplicate what I accomplished. I never had one lunch. Never did I utter one word about what I did or how I did it; not one. Until a good friend and mentor Bruce Norris called and asked me as a personal favor; if I would please divulge my strategies for becoming so wealthy so fast at an event he was planning.

As a matter of fact, most of the book you're about to read is based on the very first time I spoke before an audience of real estate investors at the first ever Millionaire Maker seminar series presented by Bruce Norris.

Investors from all parts of the country fell over themselves to grab one of those less than 300 seats which went faster than you can read the next word on this page, and why? Because with the exception of our keynote speaker, it was three days of the best presentations ever given by actual successful multi-millionaire real estate investors that actually made their money working daily in the trenches (not professional speakers or salesmen).

The first day, Bruce Norris kicked off the event with his good friend and mentor Mr. Jim Rohn, and that set the tone for what ended up being the most powerful no-nonsense event I have ever attended. Why? Because I personally witnessed some of the men and women who attended that seminar go on to become millionaires themselves in the years to follow.

That's POWERFUL!

I was fortunate enough to be the very last speaker on the very last day of that event, a day that ended with thunderous applause as everyone jumped to their feet clapping and cheering. There wasn't a dry eye in the house, and not only for me, but for the most extraordinary life-changing event they ever had the privilege of attending.

That day changed lives for those that heard the message, took it home and took action. My life as well has never been the same.

That day, I realized I had a deep desire to teach, and it awoke in me a sense of responsibility to you — that's right, YOU — that I had never felt before. And began a new part of my life which has led us to meet on the pages of this book.

You see, it's true we may not know each other yet, but by the time you finish the last word in this book we will in fact have become good friends. Do you think I'm just talking? Keep reading. You're about to learn the true secret all wealthy individuals have had to learn before they earned the right to call their own shots in this life.

I'm not sure about the next life, but in this one, if you miss this lesson, it won't matter how much money falls into your hands, it will never be enough; and most, if not all of it, will quickly be disappearing.

I'm sincerely pleased to meet you.

Now let's get moving! Time is a ticking, and you and I have got lots to do…

You're going to absolutely love this book!

Tony Alvarez

SECTION I

BREAKING INTO THE REO BUSINESS

CHAPTER 1

About the Business

What is an REO?

The term REO stands for "Real Estate Owned." It is basically an accounting term used by banks for properties that they've taken back in foreclosure. Since banks hate the term "foreclosure" (they usually like everything nice, clean and pretty), they devised an accounting term they can use in-house when discussing their non-performing assets. If you called a bank and asked for their foreclosure department, there's a very good chance they'd tell you they don't have one. REOs, or foreclosures, are something that the banks really prefer to hide. They're not very proud of their bad loans.

What Motivates Banks?

Most banks are primarily motivated by greed, not charity. All the talk we hear about banks wanting to help borrowers pay their loans is primarily motivated by making themselves look good, and pleasing their shareholders and executives. It's mostly PR. Their focus is first and foremost on increasing their gross revenues; that's it!

At the height of Wall Street's financial woes, the banks received billions in Tarp funds. And just what did they do with all our tax dollars... ?

They immediately paid themselves not millions, but BILLIONS in bonuses.

Then, they promptly invested the balance of those funds for as high a return as humanly possible.

So what's wrong with that? According to their charters, absolutely NOTHING!

That's right boys and girls, that's exactly what them good old boys are hired to do, thank God!

Because if it was any different, that would mean we would all be working for Fidel Castro cutting sugar cane in Cuba. Unfortunately, that's the price we sometimes have to pay for freedom. In other words, it's unfortunate that these guys abused our system. We can't regulate honesty, but we can punish abuses, which is what will hopefully happen as the investigations uncover fraudulent abuses.

The Truth About Banks and Lenders

Most banks and lenders are NOT interested in helping borrowers. That's nonsense. They really don't give a hoot about you or me. They just care about our money. Remember, large companies sell on what's called EBITDA (Earnings Before Interest, Taxes, Depreciation and Amortization.) Increasing their own revenue is what rings their bell.

What is REO Investing?

REO investing is basically my way of describing the fact that I focus on buying lender-owned non-performing assets, specifically one to four residential units. In all other respects, it's no different than any other kind of real estate investing. However, out of all the different types of lender-owned properties, I focus primarily on the acquisition of one to four residential dwellings. Otherwise, we're talking about basically the same buy low/sell high or hold for long-term cash flow and appreciation strategies used by most real estate investors. That's it!

Now the rest of the story...

Let's talk specifically about condition of the properties for a moment.

While occasionally some houses will be in good, even perfect condition, almost all of the properties that sell as REOs require some repairs, so be prepared.

Most will require repairs ranging from mild paint and carpet to thousands of dollars in serious fix-ups, including... electrical, plumbing, replacement of air conditioning and heating units, etc. The real dogs will require mold remediation, new windows (and I just don't mean broken glass, I mean complete installation of new windows), roofs, replacement of septic systems, replacement of main water and drain lines, and even cracked slabs.

Worst-case scenario, they will be boarded up, fire damaged, or may have already been scraped off the lot by local authorities for code violations and the banks are not even aware of it. Often, most of the appliances will be gone (cabinets, toilets, doors, windows, anything and everything that your mind can imagine).

If the previous owners were really angry, they might have even jumped up in the attic and cut all the electrical wires and broken or stolen all of the copper pipes, and you won't even know it until you turn on the water and power. I've seen everything done to these homes, everything under the sun. So make sure you inspect carefully! If you are not experienced in this area, don't worry, just find someone YOU TRUST who is.

As you can see, condition becomes the first issue you will deal with, and for many reasons, not just cost of repairs.

The level of damage will determine the type of financing you will be able to utilize when purchasing. And this will affect how you structure your offers. It's all connected.

When it comes to making offers, you have to understand what kind of financing goes with what type of house. The ones you can buy in average-to-good condition can qualify for FHA and conventional financing. Offers on dog properties, however, will require all cash or cash equivalent, meaning the use of hard-money or private investors, a fast escrow (typically from 5 to 15 days, even though in most cases the bank will not be able to perform within that time period), the seller/lenders want as clean a deal as possible so that means no contingencies and no headaches! You're buying the property as-is. No exceptions.

If it's a dog deal that turns into an ugly killer pig (meaning it has a serious hidden defect that renders the deal profitless),

it's yours! You bought it! Take it home. Hug it. Kiss it. LOVE it! You married it! BE HAPPY! and.... NEVER COMPLAIN!

Why Invest in REOs?

Personally, I've found buying REOs to be the path of least resistance. It's real, and it works!

That's it!

Now, the rest of the story ...

Investing in REOs is easier to learn and do. It's faster to get from "no money" to a good profit or cash flow. It's highly profitable, and your return on investment margins are steep. There's a huge amount of inventory; therefore, you have more selection than other times in the real estate cycle.

With REOs, you have highly motivated sellers. The banks need to dump the stuff. Prices are lower, and therefore you have lower risk.

If you fall off the second step of a 6-foot step ladder, it's less likely that you're going to get hurt and easier to get back up again than if you fall off the top step. Don't get me wrong, you can still get hurt in the REO market, but it's typically because you're not paying attention.

I don't want to mislead you. THIS IS WORK!

As a beginning investor, you may get lucky and attain a certain level of success quickly, but to make a really good, consistent amount of money in this business and hang on to it, you have to become familiar with several different elements, and you have to learn to master most of them. (None of them are all that difficult to master.) It's similar to conducting an orchestra as opposed to getting really good at playing one instrument.

Another reason I love this segment of the market is because initially you won't have much competition, and that's primarily due to fear in the marketplace. It's a little weird, but when the prices are at their lowest point, meaning when it's the easiest and most profitable time to enter a marketplace, that is typically when the majority of buyers are not buying. I've seen a lot of investors even pull away because they're afraid of what they don't know. They're afraid of what could happen. This is not, and shouldn't be, an emotionally driven part of the market. REO investing is strictly by the numbers. In other words, you don't have to worry about convincing sellers that their world is going to come to an end if they don't sell you their stuff. It's the banks you're dealing with, not homeowners. They don't get emotional about this stuff. THEY DON'T REALLY CARE!

Basically, when it comes to cutting a deal, banks function on the numbers. If a house is in average-to-fair condition and can qualify for financing, the highest offer accompanied by a good deposit, without a lot of headaches or "hair" attached, is what's going to catch their eye. Always, at the beginning of a downturn in real estate, lenders appear to favor owner-occupant offers. For the most part, this is all political rhetoric and will disappear as soon as things aren't going the way they want as fast as they want... or when they decide their public image is intact.

Remember what I mentioned about how they function and what truly motivates them. If you pay close attention, you will see just how accurate I am on this fact, and for the rest of your investment life you will be able to read a headline or hear something on the local or national news and immediately know exactly where they are signaling their next move will be.

Now, if a house is in need of serious repairs, the highest all-cash offer with no contingencies, no headaches and no problems will move to the top of the bank's list. And if it's from somebody they've done business with successfully in the past who they know is a closer, that's going to ring their bell every time.

It's pretty much a cookie-cutter system. Once you learn the steps, there's nothing simpler to manage and repeat than this business.

Why Buy Now?

This question comes up a lot: Should I get into the market now, or should I wait until the market bottoms out? The simplest answer I can give you is really a couple of questions – are you hungry or not? Can you make money right now in your chosen target market area or not? If the response to both is yes, then get going.

That's it!

Here's my point. If you're a new investor (or experienced and coming out of hibernation), there are many elements of the marketplace that you have to become familiar with, and that's an unavoidable part of the learning curve. Once you pick an area and decide how you're going to work it, what kind of inventory you want to buy, what exit strategies you will use, etc., you must overlay that on top of the reality of the marketplace. In other words, when you filter your requirements through what's happening in the marketplace, the answers will start jumping out at you. Doing this exercise will tell you if it's time for you to get in or not.

Remember this: The more you know, the more you'll make. On the other hand, the less you know, the more you will ***lose***.

Let me give you a personal example.

Because I have been investing since 1983 and analyzing my present market since 1994, I had a pretty good idea as to when it was right for me to get back into actively investing. Even though I understood that prices and rents would continue to drop, I knew I could still run a pretty good cash flow. Motivating me was the fact that I have some cash in a trust that I manage for my son and my grandson, and I MUST get the highest return possible on that money. So, when the numbers hit a certain point, that's when my bell rang!

I realized I could get a much higher return by buying single family homes and renting them out than keeping the money in anything else, including gold. That's simply what drove my decision. Sure, I knew some of the houses I would buy would continue to decline in value, but the numbers got to the point where they worked quite well even after allowing for continued decline in values and rents.

There are several benefits to being in the marketplace now. First and foremost, you own the market. And that's the way I like to think of it. You see, I sincerely believe I'm NOT the sharpest knife in the drawer. I have to work very hard at staying on top and in control of my stuff. In my mind, I have to be the most knowledgeable, most experienced and most aware investor running the best numbers in my target market. That's what sets the pattern for my decisions.

In all honesty, I want to be the top banana in the Antelope Valley bunch. That's how I have to see it in my mind.

It doesn't mean I'm right. I may not be. The truth of the matter is I may never know, because when it comes to investing, I focus 100% of my attention on my own plans, and in my mind, no one else exists.

Oh, one more thing. Don't forget, I love being loved and famous. By this I mean that by getting started early and ahead of everyone else, all of the REO agents in your target market already will have had plenty of time to fall in love with you FIRST, as they do with me, and will feel guilty about cheating on you with other, newer investors. You and I will have won their hearts and minds. And we won't have to worry about getting lost in the sea of investors that's coming.

WE WILL HAVE NO COMPETITION. I will explain the subtleties of this later in the book, just hang with me.

I want to be on the cutting edge of what's happening, and that's only possible when I'm PLAYING. You're either in or you're out. And for me, being out of the game is quite boring. That's it!

An additional motivation is the fact that with the prices we are seeing right now, I know I can make fast cash even if I just buy something, clean it up a little and then wholesale it on the MLS, or to another investor. But then again, I could just as easily completely remodel it and retail for top dollar or rent it out. It's a no-lose proposition.

Now, I don't care who you are, or where you are (even if you're at the tables in Las Vegas) when you understand that if you put some money down on a bet you're going to win, and the only question left unanswered is how much money you want to win, but win you will, heck, I'm putting my money down!

But here's the point: I don't need somebody else to prod or convince me. I've been convinced by the market. If you've already spent enough time studying the marketplace, the market will give you an indication of what to do. It will point you toward your decision. It will give you the trigger as to when to jump in.

But you have to be in first. I could go on and on about this, but what it really comes down to first and foremost is, you have to make a decision to be in!

You must commit, at least to doing the research. Once you start doing the research (pick an area, study it, decide what your exit strategies will be, etc.), the marketplace and the market data you're analyzing will seduce you into making a decision. It will quickly tell you, "You know what? Prices aren't low enough to do what you're thinking about doing. NOT HERE, AND NOT NOW." Then you have to ask yourself a new series of questions. "Well, what can I do? How can I be profitable in this marketplace right now?"

When you start playing around with those kinds of questions, you start coming up with responsible, clear-cut answers. Maybe you can wholesale the house. Maybe you can hook up with somebody else who has more experience or contacts. Maybe you can be a bird dog, finding deals where someone else has the cash, but doesn't have the time to find properties.

If you study any market long enough, the market will show you what you need to know. It delivers you to your next decision, but if you never look at it hard enough, if you never give it your attention long enough, you'll go nowhere!

Now GET MOVING!!

Erin Wicomb and Tony Alvarez

CHAPTER 2

Getting Started

First of all, let's have a meeting of the minds on just three simple but important terms.

Many times as real estate investors, we use words without really thinking about the true meaning of the actual words we're using. For example:

What is a true investor?

An investor can be described as an individual or entity that invests in assets for a specific percentage return on their investment. Typically, for a longer term and a bit more conservative.

What is a speculator?

A speculator in a financial context could be described as an entity or individual looking to receive an immediate high return on their investment capital. Usually carries a bit more risk.

What is an entrepreneur?

An entrepreneur is a person who is an ambitious leader, who combines land, labor, and capital to create and market new goods or services for a considerable risk for reward.

As you can see, these terms are different, yet they can sometimes be intermingled. But for our purposes in this book, all of these terms will represent the same meaning. By that I mean, to make it simpler for us to communicate in the pages of this book. The real estate investor, speculator and entrepreneur will all have the same meaning. It will be referred to as "investor."

As you know, there are many different ways to find and create real estate deals. You can spend your time chasing after notices of defaults, trustee sales, probates, divorces, bankruptcy filings, newspaper ads, for sale by owners, desperate sellers, and calling people and going over to their houses to try to convince them to sign over their deed and hand you the equity in their property for a few thousand bucks. You can place or scan ads on the internet (like Craig's List, real estate blogs, chat rooms and online real estate investor clubs.)

You can send out letters to absentee owners and try to do rent-to-own (lease with option to buy) or owner carry subject to master lease and sublease (sandwich lease), talk to banks directly, and try to get them to give you a good deal on their foreclosure properties, or you can try doing short sales. You can hire people as bird dogs to find you vacant houses, like the UPS guy or other people that drive around all day for a living. Man, I get tired just thinking about this stuff! It's really endless. I bet for every hair on your head, I'm sure you could find a different way of tracking down deals. Oh yeah, and don't forget auctions. As some of you already know, those can be so much fun. Many of you attended some of them. Aren't they fun? I'm sure you walked away with a great experience.

Right now a lot of this stuff is nonsense and, in my opinion, a complete waste of your time and money, especially in this segment of the real estate cycle.

Sure. You can make money doing all that stuff at some point in the real estate cycle. I know. I've done them all. I actually bought several houses at auctions myself and re-sold them quickly for a quick $20,000 profit last year. But really, do you want to chase your tail around like a mad dog? All that stuff is a lot of work. As I have mentioned to you before, I'm pretty lazy, and I'm not lying when I say that. I'm actually competing for the title of Laziest Guy on Earth. I know that about myself. Then add to that the fact that I don't consider myself to be all that bright. The point is I don't like to waste my time with nonsense just to maybe get a couple of deals every once in a while. I prefer to focus most of my attention and my consistent efforts on finding deals in a segment of the real estate market I know I can control and have it pay off consistently for the rest of my life.

I read a book by Robert Kiyosaki called *Who Took My Money?* I suggest you get it, because it's pretty good. There is a line in there where he goes to his rich dad and says, "What advice can you give me if I want to be a successful investor? What can I do? What should I shoot for?"

His rich dad says, "You should shoot to be lazy and incompetent." I read that and thought, "That's me! That's why I'm so successful!" I'm not competing with you brilliant guys. I'm taking the slow boat, and I mean it's really slow.

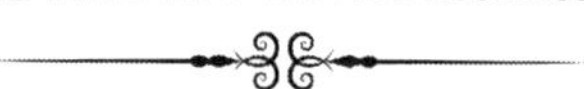

I went from bankruptcy in 1995 to $7.2 million in seven years. I did it by creating three relationships with professional agents that specialize in handling REOs and distressed situations. And people just like them are in your neighborhood right now waiting to hear from you.

If you're reading this book, you're probably a different cut of investor. And you probably already know that we have to do our business with integrity or we will fall away. Integrity and honesty are probably the two things that have added to my success more than anything else.

The only reason someone will come back to do business with you, like you will go back happily to do business with someone else, is if they treat you with respect and dignity whether you're buying a used car or putting your kid through school.

With that said, I want to go to my material and get through the details of what I did. It's so simple that I hope I don't put you to sleep.

I had a cover made up showing a silhouette of a guy holding a huge bag of money over his head. This is basically what this business is about for me. It's kind of like an agent and what an agent means to me. That's what these houses that I bought represent to me.

It's basically like this. This guy is Mr. Agent. This bag full of money represents the profit on a house. If you could see a house somehow in that bag of money, that's what it represents to me. Whenever an agent calls me, the only thing I'm thinking about is that he's handing me a bag of money and I have to do whatever it takes to make it easy for him to want to call me first — not just call me, but call me first.

Steve and Robyn Love and Tony Alvarez

CHAPTER 3

THE PATH OF LEAST RESISTANCE

Because I'm not that bright and I'm really lazy, I do things in the most simple of ways. I find the easiest way to achieve my goals. That's why this chapter is called "The Path of Least Resistance."

This really is for me, and I think you'll find it will be for you as well, the path of least resistance.

To begin with everything I do must fit into one of the following three categories:

1. The Goal which is basically where we're going to go. You've heard a lot about goals.

2. The Plan which is the method I'm going to use. It's simple. Buy low, sell high or rent.

3. The Systems which are the daily action steps I must take to implement my plan and ultimately reach my goal.

I refer to this as my personal G.P.S.® (Goal, Plan, Systems).

I'm going to cover those things with you. Then we'll cover what I did, but that was a while ago, from '95 until probably four years ago. I've been sitting back like you would not believe! I try to lay out by the pool when it's winter.

Then, because I got bored, I started doing some of what other people do, mailing out letters and all this. I've had my poor son sending out 2,000 letters a week. It's made my life interesting, I have to admit. I can't tell you how much I respect these guys who find deals using other methods every day, because it's work. It pays off, though.

We started doing those letters four months ago. My son just came into the business. I messed up two deals. One had an $85,000 profit. The other one had $75,000 profit. My son was looking at me saying, "And you're going to train me in this business? You don't mind if I call some of these guys you talk about instead?"

I said, "No. We'll get the hang of it."

He said, "Let's go to a cheaper neighborhood, someplace where it won't matter if we screw up."

We locked up four. I think the smallest profit we're going to make is $50,000. I thought, "I'm really stupid. I could have been doing this the whole time, along with these three agents that were delivering this inventory to me."

I attended Bruce Norris's boot camp with Charles Harris, a very successful investor in California. I remember Charles couldn't make it one day because he was out doing something else. I was thinking, "He's nuts. Look at the money we paid. I'm in here until he throws me out." Then I went home from that place and went right back to doing what I do. I called my agents and talked to them. "How are you doing? How's your family?"

Charles went out and took action and made money. I know Charles doesn't like to talk about numbers. He keeps things kind of sealed up, but I extracted this data from him. He made somewhere in the vicinity of $400,000 in three or four months. When I heard that I almost jumped out of my own skin.

I was there. I heard the same things. I went home and did nothing. He went home and went to work. He even admitted that most of what he did wasn't the right thing. He did it by accident.

I told Bruce that up until now I thought he was smart. Sometime during that seminar, I was sitting back there and I realized he's a genius. He really is. There is something in this guy that knows how to put these little pieces together to make something better than the individual pieces.

You're going to learn a lot from this book, but if you don't do something with it, five months from now you'll meet someone else who read this same book, took action and made a half a million dollars. And you'll be there scratching your head thinking, "What did I miss?"

Don't just read this book. When you're done reading it, follow it up by taking some real action!

Rina and Tony Alvarez

CHAPTER 4

The Goal

There I was, out of bankruptcy at the LA Courthouse. They took my Corvette, which I had no business buying to begin with. I was paying $450 a month and couldn't afford that. I had to walk home to Burbank. That's about 25 miles, so I had a lot of time to think about what I would or wouldn't do again in my business life.

I got a part-time job at a pizza place. They gave me a bow tie and a little orange hat. I looked like Porky Pig, but I learned to make great pizzas. I learned you can go to the salad bar and put all that stuff on your pizzas. They weren't on the menu, but people would come in and say, "Can I get bacon on mine? I saw you putting bacon on yours." Now it's a regular thing. You see how the word spreads?

My original goal was $1 million. That takes guts. I didn't even have a car. The only reason I got the job at the pizza place was because it was within walking distance to my home. That's the only reason. My goal was $1 million in five years with a $10,000 monthly net income. At the time it was, "My God, but I'm going to do it!" That was it.

How was I going to do it? My plan was to buy little houses at 50% below the after-repair market value (ARV). My selling and holding costs were 10% to 15% of the after-fix-up value. I used that retail value as the mark. My selling costs were 10% to 15%. You can crisscross those numbers any way you want.

CHAPTER 5

The Plan

My whole plan was buy, fix, sell and move on as fast as I could. I did that for a while, but because I came out of bankruptcy, I had a $500,000 tax loss carry forward to write-off against new income. If you understand taxes and losses, I had no motivation to keep anything because I wanted to churn and burn that tax loss as quickly as I could.

At the same time I wanted to build up my cash stores, and I was broke. I borrowed $6,000 from my father, who had more love for me than sense at the time because if he had really thought about it, he would never have given me the money.

One day, I was reading the paper while at the library. It said the Antelope Valley had become the foreclosure capital of the United States, much like Sacramento, California and Orlando, Florida are today, so I started out. After doing some initial research and confirming the fact that it was, in fact, a disaster zone, I decided to move to the Antelope Valley because I could be a big fish in a small pond. Three-bedroom houses previously valued at over $100,000 were selling for $30,000. One of the things I used in my evaluation of the area was to calculate what it would cost to replace the homes that were selling for $30,000.

For the first house I bought, I paid $37,000. It was a three-bedroom, one-bath, and was about 1,000 square feet. I figured out that at that precise moment in time it would cost $75,000 to build that house. I thought, "This is a no-brainer." I repaired that house for about $4,000 and sold it for $60-plus thousand. I kept doing that until I used up that $500,000 tax loss.

How did I do it? I chose to work with real estate agents that controlled inventory. During those years, just like now, there were hundreds of properties in foreclosure. The agents that represent these companies all have their own stalls of investors, men and women they've been dealing with for years. They have relationships with them. How do I get my foot in the door? They've been working with these people. They trust them. My challenge was to answer the question, how do I get my foot in the door? But really, the deeper question was why would they want to work with me?

The house thing, fixing them up, was not a challenge. That's easy. So was finding the deals; they were everywhere. You could trip over boarded-up houses. I realized that I had to get to those people somehow. I had to get them to work with me. What was the magic bullet? We'll get to that.

Those are the basic details of my goals and my plan. Here is a general idea of the systems I used then. I pretty much use the same systems today, but I do them a little differently.

CHAPTER 6

The Systems

I contacted agents on a weekly basis. I didn't just do real estate agents and brokers. I also found it was beneficial for me to do the same thing with my insurance agent, the hard-money lender I decided to work with, and the title representative I used.

I found by accident I was practicing my relationship building skills with them. They're people that kind of matter, but if you lose that relationship you can get another one right away. You can't mess with the agent relationship at all.

On a weekly basis, 70% of my time would go into an outreach program. I would call and visit them. Thirty percent went into dealing with fixing up the properties, managing them, getting rid of them, and doing whatever I had to do. Remember at the beginning I was buying and selling, buying and selling; there was no property management at all.

I used hard-money lenders and investors for my financing, but I quickly figured out that it was far more beneficial for me to have a hard-money lender who would respect me than to align myself with other investors who were always challenging me on my decisions, and I had to pay them more. I had to give them half of what I earned to listen to them tell me how to do the stuff I already knew how to do.

I hired workers as employees to do the repair cost. I did this because I had so much inventory coming in. Some months, I would buy five to 10 houses. Once you get that pipeline going, you have to have your own workers. Contractors are bad enough when you only have one or two houses being repaired. You're always waiting for them to show up and do what they have to do. When you have 10 houses, you're churning and burning and relisting them, you have to find a way to do that. That's what I chose to do, but you have to have enough inventory to justify that decision.

I had one office assistant. I have never had more than that. You can set things up so they work very efficiently. To be honest with you, I think they work probably 50% of the time. The rest of the time they're looking at you saying, "I'm not reading. I'm really not looking at this magazine. I was just thumbing through it." In other words, they have a lot of time.

I outsource the bookkeeping and tax preparing. I'm terrible with all that kind of stuff. I give it to people that know what they're doing, and I don't think about it. I don't want to think about it. I know we should really get involved a little more, but I hate it. I'm not competent in that area.

If the volume gets really high, an assistant to handle follow-up with your agents and brokers is not a bad way to go. However, the bad news is you won't be able to find one. I found one person. He has very similar character traits to my own. That's why I loved him.

But, because he's so good at what he does, eventually he went on his own.

Once you train somebody and they have it, how much are you going to pay them to stay? "Here, take half of what I make." "No." "Take three-quarters." "No... you'd better leave because you can do it on your own." He was wonderful. I really miss him because he was really good.

I averaged four to 10 purchases per month. My closing percentage was 100%. I just threw that in there for the heck of it because it sounds good, but it's a given. In this business you won't be negotiating. All the negotiating skills you may have learned along the way won't help you here. Why?

Agents do the negotiating for you once you develop a relationship. At the beginning, they'll be treating you like any other buyer. "The house is listed for $200,000." You know that fixed up it's worth $100,000 more. You say, "I'd like to buy it from you." They say, "Make an offer. Get in line. We have 17 other offers already." "Well, I want to use you. You're the listing agent." They say, "No problem. It's going to have to be full price or maybe higher."

Once you develop a relationship with them, it will go from that kind of a situation to this kind of phone call. Your phone rings. You pick it up. You know it's the agent because you looked at your cell phone and you know their numbers already. Don't pretend you don't know. You say, "Hey, John. How's it going? What's happening?"

"I have five properties coming down the line. They're not on the MLS yet. I have the addresses in my office. Four of those are right over the plate for you. Here's the number you have to hit to make this deal happen." All the time this is going on, I'm by the pool. It doesn't get any better than that. There's no negotiating. There's nothing.

I have to tell you that because I'm not so bright, I would push the envelope. "Can't we get another $5,000 off that $35,000 house?" when I knew it was worth $75,000. These were the prices back then. "Can we just squeeze that down?"

I would hear laughter on the phone, because now they know me. They would say, "I can't believe you're even asking me the question!" Sometimes it did work, though. I actually bought some houses for $12,000. You can't buy anything for $12,000.

Sabrina Gaunce and Tony Alvarez at Tony's office

SECTION I: PART 1

PERFORMANCE

"I know the price of success: dedication, hard work and an unremitting devotion to the things you want to see happen."

- Frank Lloyd Wright

Bruce Norris, Tony Alvarez and Mike Cantu

CHAPTER 7

A Series of Firsts

I'm going to talk to you about a series of firsts. I want you to pay attention to a lot of the stuff I say. It is so light and airy, and some distinctions may seem so basic that you may miss the importance of them.

Some of it is subtle, and you may miss the value in it. I find that it's those subtle things that make the difference between making just one or two million (which would have been okay, I would have hit my goal and I would have been fine) and making some bigger bucks.

First, let's talk about finding the agents.

CHAPTER 8

Finding the Agents

There are a few basic ways to find REO agents. If you have access to the Multiple Listing Service (MLS), you can put in catch words like:

- Fannie Mae
- Freddie Mac
- Bank-owned
- Lender-owned
- Fixer-upper
- REO
- Corporate-owned
- Etc…

It will pull up the actual listings and tell you who the agent is. Everybody understands that.

If you don't have access to the MLS, but have access to the internet, go to www.FannieMae.com or www.reobroker.com, www.nrba.com, www.assignreo.com, www.car.org, or www.realtor.org and look for agents and properties in your area. They'll list properties they have for sale, and will have information about the agents representing the properties within those given areas. It also lets you know if there are any properties available for sale in your local investment area.

You can also find agents on various websites which are listed under the resource section of this book. These sites are specifically designed to list REO and other agents. Use them!

A very simple and unsophisticated method of finding agents within a specific area I am interested in (and one that I still use today, for finding agents that specialize in handling distressed properties) is to drive around your target market neighborhoods and call on all the available listings. This gives me a chance to speak to them about a specific house that they have for sale, and get my foot in the door, even if the listing is already pending or sold. I use it as an icebreaker.

CHAPTER 9

Sell Us Your Dogs

Here's a simple, cost-effective marketing technique I used that worked for me. I learned this from a good friend and investor I met years ago (who I love) while working as a real estate appraiser, Bill Swift. Billy is a genius, but he doesn't know it yet. He is Mr. Knowledgeable, a no-nonsense kind of guy, and he's presently working with his lovely wife, Pam. They are brokers and run a very successful business in the Apple Valley in Southern California. His website is chock-full of free analytical data on his area (www.wiestrealty.com). The website is also listed in the resource section of the book.

I highly recommend you check out their website even if you're from elsewhere in the country, because it will help you to learn the type of info you should be focused on in order to be a successful long-term player in your area. Now, back to Billy's idea. It takes more effort and produces less, but I target it to newer agents. I found that newer agents somehow, and I really didn't synthesize why, were able to come up with deals that sometimes they didn't really know what they had in their hands. Some were representing smaller lenders or somebody who they knew, like a friend or family member, who was in default or financial trouble.

We put flyers together. The heading on my flyer started with, "Sell us your dog properties" (see Appendix D). We started delivering these flyers to the individual real estate offices and requested that they put them on their agents' desks.

I also used title reps. Title reps have to market their services to real estate agents. They go to the agents' offices every day and know who is a pro and who is a part-time agent; who is the hot new agent and who is doing real estate as a hobby.

This was another effective way of marketing I did, and it paid my rent. Those deals did come in. Today we do the same thing. We just added email as the mode of delivery. You can get access to all the agents' email addresses listed at your local board of realtors. They love email.

I want you to remember that all marketing should have at least two goals within the message:

1. To solicit a direct response from your target audience

2. To keep yourself or your company in the minds of potential clients or associates who may need your services in the future or who can refer you to someone they know.

Now imagine wrapping that flyer up in some important article or message to help an agent acquire knowledge or put more money in his pocket in something they receive from you every week. Imagine the cumulative effect that will have for relationship building.

That's a simple technique, but be careful not to abuse it or break the commandment, "Thou shall not waste an agent's time with nonsense." I find the best information to pass on is informative, educational, inspirational and motivational.

CHAPTER 10

Calling the Agent

Once you go into one of those services and find a specific listing, whether you get it off the MLS or from the internet, you want to call that agent and start your conversations about that specific listing. You don't want to go in and say, "I'm an investor and I'm going to make your life wonderful. I'm going to buy a bunch of properties from you. I'm really geared up and have money." At that moment, you don't want to give them that song-and-dance routine.

This is crucial. Your first words to him are going to set the tone for how he thinks about you. You have to be aware of this. If you talk to him about something that means something to him, you have gone a little further than 90% of the other people that want the house that are investors or wannabe investors.

If you start the conversation with, "How you doing, John? This is Tony. I have some money and want to buy some fixer-uppers. If you deal with me you're going to have it made, because I'm going to buy 10 a month," his eyes will be rolling in his head, "Another seminar graduate!" They don't really respect us. You have to earn that respect.

You start the conversation with a particular listing. Say, "Give me the details." Ask the usual questions. Ask the questions about the property, and then introduce yourself after that.

I'm going to break this conversation down for you.

Somewhere in that conversation after they're giving you the details on a specific property, a concern is going to run across that agent's mind. That concern is, "Do you really understand what you're buying? Am I wasting my time on this phone call with you?" He or she is going to say to you, "You know this property needs some repairs. Have you got cash? You have to really know what you're doing."

What has that done? That has opened the door for you to come back to him and say, "I'm an investor." Now he's at ease. Notice the subtle difference between responding to his concern about your ability to perform as opposed to you calling him and out of the gate saying, "Hi, I'm an investor."

You have the same amount of money in your bank account, but he's not aware of it. He's talking to you on the phone. He doesn't know if you have $1 million. You may well have $10 million cash that you have access to. He has no clue. How you communicate with that agent on the call is going to make a world of difference.

Why? Because you're looking for his response, and you want him to love you as soon as possible. By the way, that four-letter word is going to be thrown around a lot in this book because I believe that love is at the center of the success I've had with all these guys. They truly love me, and I love them. I can't tell you how much. Wouldn't you love somebody who makes you $7.2 million?

After all, I have a family member I love and he's only cost me money.

When you're having that conversation, you have to get a feel for that agent's personality. That's a simple statement, but I think you guys know what I'm saying. You'll know if he's rude, impatient, polite, helpful, irritated, whatever. However, I have to tell you about one of the first REO agents I met who over time has become one of my best personal friends. Because I would have never guessed that's how we would have ended up based on how we started out -- the guy who's responsible for 50% of the $7.2 million I've made.

Because my last name is Alvarez, when I call on the phone in an area out there in the desert and say, "Hi, my name is Tony Alvarez," they have a picture in their mind of who Tony Alvarez is based on the last movie they saw. I'm sure I would have gotten a different response if I called up with a heavy Spanish accent and said, "Hi. I'm Tony Alvarez. I am from Cuba and I'm an investor. I'm going to buy all the stuff you've got out there. I drove by the house and it's a disaster. You can't sell that to anybody. You're lucky I called you."

From the phone call, he already has a preconceived notion about "Alvarez." I'm a fruit picker, and his parents told him somewhere along the line that I'm not as valuable.

Now, you get a chance to do two things. One, you get a chance to learn something about yourself. Two, you get a chance to teach him something about him. And if you do these things effectively, you have harpooned the whale, and you will drive that harpoon deep into him.

Think about it. Do you have access to capital? Can you hire a contractor to fix a house? Do you think you can talk to an agent, find a house, and fix it up? Do you think you can accomplish that? Can you buy a house? Can you fix it? Can you call an agent and sell it? He's going to get paid a commission, right? The point is that because people get paid when these things happen, they're really not that hard to get accomplished.

Let's do a little change. Suppose the agent controlling that inventory is my dad or my son or a good friend who really cares about me, and I'm also an investor. You can all compete with me. You may be better than me. You may have 10 times my cash. You could have 100 times the intelligence.

You may be a contractor and get the work done lickety-split while I'm arguing with Fernando and Mario that work for me. I love them both. Without them, I'd be in trouble. You can do all that stuff. In that area, in the performance area of this business, you can compete with me from here to doomsday, but in the relationship area, my relationship with Don Anderson, with Charla Abbot, with J.C. Boucher is mine. I own it. You cannot touch it.

But here's the good news. You can do the same thing I've done. You can build your own relationship, and with exactly the same people. And I (or anybody else) can't interfere with that bond. Did you understand what I said? If you have someone in your life you care about, whether it be your mother, brother, sister, friend, doctor, or even the FedEx guy, it doesn't matter who it is, your relationship with that person is just between you and them. If you have more than one child, you're lucky because you'll understand this right away. You love them both, but those relationships are completely different. Respect that knowledge. That will make a difference in this business.

CHAPTER 11

Interviewing the Agent

Try to get a feel for the agent. Are they friendly, hostile, dry, a control freak, knowledgeable? Establish rapport by asking questions about the real estate market and their opinion. Real estate agents, like all of us, like to talk about what we know. Ask them in that first conversation. You talk about their listing. Once you realize they've given you all their information and are running out of steam (because they can't keep their attention on you forever on that phone call), you have to be ready. Re-energize their mind by taking them in a different direction.

You have to say, "What do you think is going on in the market?" Give them time to respond to you, and use their brain to think in response to your questions. Be interested in their opinions. What does this do? It just creates a little conversation, rapport, between you guys. It starts to develop a relationship. It will be the best opportunity for you to say, "How about meeting in your office?" For me, personal, face-to-face meetings are crucial.

I will tell you something interesting. You will learn every time you do something. Every time I speak at some meeting or class, it never fails; someone always comes up and says, “Hey, I’m a little worried. I don’t think I can do what you do. I don’t do well with personal contacts.” What they’re really saying is a lot of different things, but at the heart of it they’re saying, “I don’t know that people are going to like me. How do I get over that hurdle?” Some of this has some psychological basis.

But here’s the thing. Do you have any idea that the agent who controls that inventory is thinking the same things as you are? We’re not all that different. Some of us feel a little more confident about ourselves than others, based on what we know. Take us out of that area and we’re falling all over ourselves.

Jack Fullerton and Tony Alvarez
Millionaire Maker Seminar

CHAPTER 12

My First Encounter "I'm a fruit Picker"

Take the first agent I met. Do you want to know what he said to me the very first time we met? I walked into his office without an appointment, which is what I'm getting to here. They said, "Tony Alvarez is up front waiting for you."

He comes around the corner. He's a tall man, as white as white can be. I can tell this is a "good ol' boy." He has a big smile. When he comes around the corner, he is looking for his version of Tony Alvarez. He looks right past me because I don't fit the bill I look more like him. Heaven only knows the picture in his mind as to what I am supposed to look like... maybe Scarface, a gardener, or the guy at the drive-up window asking, "Do you want fries with that?" Unfortunately, that's what this world does to us. Once he realized it was me, this is straight out of his mouth, "Whoa! I thought you were going to be dark with kinky hair!"

This is a crucial moment for you if you're in my shoes.

Here's a chubby, short white guy looking more like him, and I don't have any slang or any Spanish accent in my speech. I'm speaking clear English. I took that in the vein you should take it, which is it automatically let me know his level of knowledge, his life experiences, what his beliefs are to a certain extent, and his limitations.

Learn to do that. Learn to figure out what's coming out of somebody's mouth, and what those words really represent, and you will control that relationship.

We're not talking about manipulation. I am not talking about that. That does not impress me. I don't want to have anything to do with it. I get bored when somebody starts talking about that kind of stuff.

What I'm talking about is the same thing you do in your home with your family. You think about what you're going to talk to your kids about. You want a certain end result, and you think about how to approach it. That's what it's about.

Are you all wondering what I said in response to his comment? I have to tell you, I was shocked. I was smiling at him. Some of the things that ran across my mind I can't say here, but I thought them with a smile.

I want you to understand that it wasn't the first time in my life that had happened, so I had a little bit of training. I've been dealing with that stuff since I was a kid. My family, having come here from Cuba, was the first Spanish-speaking family to ever land in Lawrence, Massachusetts. As I grew up, I learned this language, and trained myself not to let my Spanish accent crawl in and let everybody know where I came from.

I used to get jabbed in the ribs by the kids saying, "Look at them damned Cubans moving into the neighborhood. Did you see the Cubans?" I'd say, "I don't know. Looks like they're taking over. We'd better move." I used to get, "Are you Italian?" I'd say, "I'm Italian, I'm Irish, I'm whatever the heck you want me to be."

I grew up in a neighborhood that was half Italian, half Irish. There were a couple of French guys, and one Jewish kid I became fast friends with. It's obvious why. He was one of my best buddies. He used to say to me, "You Cubans are the Jews of the Caribbean."

Now back to that first agent. My response to him was, "No. No, I know I really don't look Hispanic. Isn't that something?" I then reached over and put my hand on his shoulder and said, "You know what? I thought you were going to look completely different, too. As a matter of fact, you look a lot like John Wayne." We both broke out into laughter and then he said the magic words, "The conference room is busy. Why don't we go into my personal office?" Zing! And I'll tell you why that's a zing.

If I had gone into that conference room, what would I learn about this guy? Absolutely zero. I'm not going to learn anything in there. I'm going to learn he has a conference room. It has great chairs. Maybe I won't even fit in his chairs. If it's got arms, I'm worried already. "No, I'll just stand. I've been sitting in my car all day because if I sit in it, I may have to take the chair with me!"

When we get in his office, what do you think was hanging on the wall? A picture of John Wayne, right next to everything else he loves. Honestly, I'm surprised I didn't see some Cuban's head on a mantel. "I got him down in Florida. It took me one shot, right between the eyes. Dropped him like that!"

Keep one thing in mind, and I'll remind you of this later on. I love him. He loves me. He's one of my best friends. I think you will be surprised at where the relationship went. I'm responsible for 50% of that occurring. He's responsible for making me filthy rich. He made me loaded. And I am loaded. I have bucks. I scare myself sometimes. I kept thinking, "I'm too stupid to have all this money!" It's a self-esteem thing.

Nick Manfredi and Tony Alvarez

CHAPTER 13

First Office Visit

Now let's get back to getting you inside an agent's office for an appointment. This is your best opportunity. For example, you could say, "I know you're busy, but maybe I could drop by to meet with you later today or tomorrow for just a minute." If you ask him for an appointment and he does not give you one because, remember, he's not respecting you right now, drop into that agent's office two days later.

Why? I don't have a clue. All I know is that if you go to three days, he won't even remember the call. If you show up the first day, he's going to get upset because you came in without an appointment. There's something about the two-day thing.

You can get away with walking in there in two days and saying, "Can I speak with Mike?" Jerry, John or whoever it is, to the girl up front. And while you're at it, you had better be nice to whoever you meet in that office the minute you walk through that door. It wouldn't hurt you to have something in your hands like chocolate. I'm a huge fan of chocolate.

I don't mean walk in there eating a Snicker's bar. The lady's not going to say, "Can I have a bite?" I have found that receptionists love candy. They love chocolates. And if there's anybody in that office getting abused, she's at the front counter. You've got to learn to love those people because when the big guy in the back office doesn't feel like talking to you she'll say, "I'm sorry, Mr. Agent is not in right now." "This is Tony Alvarez." "Tony, he's having a slice of pizza in the kitchen. He doesn't want to be bothered." "Please let him know I called." "Got it, Big T!" I will get through that shell. I will get to the agent and get his attention, and it's because I've brought her chocolate and I treat her with dignity and respect. And those two words will come up a lot.

Now you're in the office. You drop in without an appointment within two days. They're going to love you. You're in there looking around and seeing everything. Pay attention in that first meeting. Take mental notes, but don't bring a pad and start writing down, "He loves football." Just make a cursory review. We're all pretty bright, and you're going to do this.

Make conversation on what you see, and ask questions. Now is the time to make a connection.

Look up at his walls when you get that little space or air gap to say something. He has a plaque there about softball. You see one for every year for the last 10 years. He doesn't have another one because there's no more room on his wall. It might be a good idea to ask him about it. Ask the agent, "Do you love softball that much? I donate money, too. I get those all the time." He says, "Yes

I donate money to that. My daughter does that, and my son does this. I love that. I love getting out there and getting involved."

Later, I found out that the agent (the same agent who gave me a hard time about being Hispanic) spends a lot of time helping minorities. Somewhere along the line, he is trying to bridge something in his path. He's trying to find a way through his own life. It came out that he's very active in different things. This is a real man who cares about things in his life just like you and me and those things move him.

Do you think that I ended up at some point donating money to any of those softball teams, for goodness sake? I own them. A lot of the money donated was not in my name. It was in his name. You want to talk about winning the hearts and minds of somebody who can make you rich! I just spend a few hundred bucks... every month.

Make conversations and ask questions. Now is the time to make a connection. I really mean that. You want to have something in common with him or learn something from him, which is even better. If you don't know anything about something on his wall, ask the question, "What the heck is that? I'm just curious. It looks beautiful."

Sabrina Gaunce, Tony Alvarez and Sam Green

CHAPTER 14

Tools of the Trade

This is the meeting. Bring your resume. Here's the thought I want you to remember: You want to be hired as an investor. Those are the tools of the trade. I never leave home without them. If you have a wad of cash in your bank statement, brag about it. Just don't brag about it to somebody who's going to hold you up.

The tone of this meeting is to impress the heck out of this guy or gal. As you're going to find out, I say "guy" a lot, but I work with both. They have both equally made me loaded.

Get a letter of credit from your lender like The Norris Group. Not all hard-money lenders are created equal. You need to get a letter from a company that knows how to structure a letter of credit for the bank. (See Appendix B.) If you can, get them to give you one of those letters that says you're approved for such-and-such amount of money. It's based on everything, including giving you a physical. Get it, and take it with you. It will show that you're a cut above the other investors that are going to be calling and trying to compete with you. They're trying to impress the same agent on the phone with empty promises while you're putting stuff in front of them in your first meeting. You're closing this guy. You're letting him know you're going to do business. And while you're at it, give them evidence of past performance.

If you have a 1031 exchange happening or have completed transactions, show them. If you have an active one, that's even better. He knows you're on the hook right now. You have to move. You have 45 days to close the deal.

An inventory of existing properties you own will build credibility. I'm laughing at myself. When I met Bruce Norris, I had my spreadsheet. I went to his office the first time and put all these spreadsheets in front of him. I carry them with me all the time. I use them to show people what I've paid for them, the date I bought them, when I sold them, how much I made, and what my net income was. It helps them to know about you. Keep track of every deal you make. It's worth gold!

Everybody says, "Familiarity breeds contempt." To me, familiarity removes doubt and creates confidence. The more they get to know you, the easier it's going to be for them to say, "I want to work with you."

When they understand you and know you better and they've done a few deals with you, if it's between you and the other guy they've known for 10 years, with whom they may have some bad history that's going to make a difference.

I want you to know this right now. The investors that are in their stall, the other 5, 10 or 35 guys they've been working with for years, they're delivering deals right into their hands. And yet none of them ever took the time to do any of the things I'm telling you to do. If they had, I would not have made the $7.2 million.

Explain things to the agents you start working with. A verbal resume goes along with your written information. Talk to them about yourself. Talk to them about other agents in the area that you've done deals with. Agents in this field don't compete. They cooperate. They all know each other, and they all talk. If there is anybody you've done a deal with, drop that name to him or her. They'll think, "They're okay if Jerry worked with them." They almost feel a little competitive and want to steal you away from the other agent.

All of these things are important. They all give you credibility. All you're trying to do is build credibility.

Explain your plans. If you're looking to build long-term relationships, explain that after you've spent some time with them. Let your hair down. He's let his hair down. You know a little bit about his life. Let him know this is where you're going. I'm famous for this in my area. I will take that to the last degree.

You want to get them on board with you! You want them to believe you're going somewhere. That will help them to open up to you. They want to be with winners. They don't want to be with a guy who's going to get them into escrow and then cancel. You're going to find out that's death for an agent and could ultimately lose them the multi-million dollar account!

CHAPTER 15

First Call From the Agent

Let's say you got to this point; meaning they have a deal and they call you. Speed is everything here. You have to move. Respond immediately and with confidence. Get back to them the same day.

Do not expect a great deal on the first call. The deal they are going to give you is the one that nobody wanted. You're going to get the dog or pig property that all his regular investors rejected.

Here's what also happens. Sometimes it will be a good deal, but the other investors are too busy, for one of many reasons. I've been on the receiving end of that situation. I've had 20 rehabs going at one time. They call me up and say, "Hey, I've got another two houses." I know if I take them, they're going to take eight months to complete. I may be able to close the deal, but I'm going to be paying interest on a loan on a vacant house that could be vandalized or burned down by kids or vagrants.

They're going to call you on this property. It's the worst one. All the other investors saw it.

I want you to know something else. Many times, that property has been listed for a little while. You're not paying attention to the

MLS. If there was a mistake I made, that would be it. At first, I didn't follow the MLS on a consistent basis. After I learned from these mistakes, I monitored the MLS three times a day.

They call and give you this address. You go out and it's the worst thing you've ever seen. It's a disaster. You look at it and get angry. You can't even believe this guy would call you. You can't wait to pick up the phone and sarcastically let him know it.

But the worst mistake you can make is no call at all. You just write it off.

In your mind, you think, "I can't make a profit on this thing." You don't want to call the guy back because you don't want to tell him no. You think, "I'll just ignore it. Somebody else will buy it before I have to. Then I'll get back to him in a couple of days."

If you do that, you've lost everything you've built. If you've built any credibility with that agent, you have now lost it.

You want to get back to him immediately. If you can, call him back that hour. You want to say, "I went by the house. It looks like this. I can do it. Let's move." If you can't do it, you want to go to his office and explain to him why you couldn't. That's going to set the tone for any other calls you get, if you ever get one.

You don't want to complain. I'll tell you why I know this. I am a professional complainer. I was the guy who would call him up right away and say, "Are you kidding me?" That's a dump! I can't make any money on that house. Not at that price." Never do that. Never complain! Never complain! Never complain. But never buy a deal (even your first) if it has no profit, thinking it will help make a connection with the agent, because it won't. Not one bit!

In the real estate marketplace, you have all kinds of investors involved, but there's one thing we all have in common. We buy and sell property for profit. If you can't make a profit on that house, no one can. This is what has to happen. Don't buy that deal.

Go back to that agent and say, "John, I need to talk to you because I'm concerned about something. This the first deal you gave me. I don't want you to think I didn't take the time to go out there, see the house and do my due diligence. I want you to sit with me and give me five minutes. I want to explain the situation I have. It's really causing me some stress."

You take him into his conference room. You sit down and show him what your fix-up cost is. Maybe you saw that the house has a cracked slab, the septic tank is open, and it's underneath a patio. The electric meter has been removed by code enforcement, and now you have to deal with the city. Show him the numbers and tell him, "These are the reasons I can't do this deal at this price, BUT..."

Here are some magic words for you. Say, "But if you can help me make sense of this deal, I will buy it."

"If you can help me, I will buy it." What's the only thing he can do for you? Get the price lowered. That's it! And that's all you need to make it into a profitable deal, but here's the difference (and the crucial part of what I'm telling you here today.) Do you think any of the other 35 investors ever came in to see him with their statistics and explained things to the agent in detail? Heck no! They're out fixing houses. They're out doing things. To them, that's just a phone call. They pick up the phone and say, "Hey John, that's a dog property. Forget it. I'm not dealing with that. The price is too high." His response is, "Yes, the price is too high. Goodbye."

The other half of the investors he works with didn't even call him. They just blew him off. They know that he knows it's a waste of time at that price. It's been in the MLS and every other investor saw it. All the other agents have seen it. Nobody bought it. It's sitting there. Everybody is laughing at each other. That's the conversation in the office.

But here's the thing (and believe me when I tell you), you're going to be the only one on his mind when he gets that lowered. Why? You said, "I'll buy it." Inside, he's going to be slightly ticked off at all the guys who blew him off and didn't call him back. That's just human nature.

Now, look—on the performance side of the business, we all compete. We can all do the same thing. He knows it, but he's going to choose the guy that left an impression. Remember, it's up to you to follow up, "Hey John, what happened with that deal? Did they lower it yet?" You must keep yourself on their mind.

Be thankful and gracious, whatever the outcome. Call him and say, "I appreciate you calling me and giving me the chance to go out there and try to do that deal, but this is why I can't do it." Always take the time to explain and be respectful.

Once you develop a relationship with an agent, there's no negotiating on these deals. Why? Because they know the number that's going to work with the seller; and they will lead you. Listing agents do put some research into what price to list the properties at because they want to move them quickly. If they don't, Fannie Mae will re-list the property with another agent. I'm going to get a little deeper into that because this area of the business functions like a web of contacts and connections. These agents cooperate. They don't compete.

Always perform as promised or better. You should know that by now.

After you get the deal, follow up with gratitude. Go outside the deal. Do something you're not obligated to do. Get creative. I'm not talking about handing him $500 or $5,000 cash in an envelope. That's not what I'm talking about. And just for the record, that is illegal and stupid!

By this time, you should have learned something about that agent that moves him. What I've done and suggest you do are little things. The reason they're perceived as huge is because no one else has done them. I will send him a $100 gift certificate to Outback Restaurant if I know he's a steak eater. I'll send a little note that says, "Thank you very much. I can't tell you how much I appreciate what you did," along with a fruit and pastry basket large enough for the whole office. It's a little thing, but remember—none of his other investors cared enough to do that.

It's amazing to me how in a business worth millions of dollars and in which people talk to each other and cut deals all day long, how little gratitude and respect we have for each other. It's a big part of why I'm such a success. I'm incompetent and lazy, but I know how to say thank you. That's it.

Bill Tan, Tony Alvarez, Rina Alvarez, and Bill Tan Sr.

CHAPTER 16

Getting a Second Chance on a Dog Deal

If you can't make the deal work, explain why. Show the agent it's not workable and say, "If you can help me make these numbers work, I'll buy the deal." You'll get the second chance.

The guy who has made me the most money has been in business in the Antelope Valley since 1954. Not him personally, but the father and the grandfather before him. They're known as people that have tremendous dignity and integrity. They have a great reputation as being the most experienced, knowledgeable, honest, hardworking folks in the area.

Because I associate myself with them and they accept me, when I walk into that office, I want you to know I'm treated like a king. I relate to them. I ride with them. I get that respect that they've had since 1954. I entered that place in 1996.

If Fannie Mae needs an agent, they hire them because of all the reasons I just told you. They're the oldest and the best, and they have integrity. They do a good job. Now when Fannie Mae needs another agent, where do you think they go for that other agent?

Here's Fannie Mae in their infinite wisdom. They need another agent to basically check on that first agent's performance and give a second opinion. Where do you think they are going? They go to him; the first agent.

They ask the guy they presently have approved to refer a trusted friend, "Hey, we need another agent to compete with you. Can you recommend someone?" Yes, he can. Now he has a problem. You would think this is an opportunity. He has a problem because he has to refer somebody who's going to compete with him. They may take business away. He needs a relationship with the person that is as good as with his mother. This new guy can kill his business. If he makes the wrong choice here, he's dead.

They sort of cooperate. He tells Fannie Mae, "I know the guy you need. You need this agent." He gets on the phone and calls him. He says, "Fannie Mae just told me they need another agent. I'm recommending you. Don't make me look bad."

Keep in mind that this guy has been in town for many moons. He has a lot of pull as it is. These guys are both semi-friends. They cooperate. The second guy gets the call and is approved. He's now grateful to the first referring agent. He's also an old timer. He's not going to recommend a new guy that has no loyalty, a new guy who only thinks about money, not relationships. Not all new guys are like that. He's not going to recommend a hotshot.

Now let's get back to what matters.

So watch what happens. Now, here's our listing. We can't do the deal. You came back and explained it to him. You said, "Okay, when you get the dollars right, I'm your guy. I'm going to buy this." He didn't get any calls from anybody else. Nobody wants it. It's a disaster.

He goes back to Fannie Mae and does the one thing he does not want to do. He tells Fannie Mae, "I'm sorry, but it's not selling in the MLS. It's been three weeks and everyone has seen it. We need to lower the listing price."

Fannie Mae has one of two choices. They can lower that price based on his integrity, their past relationship, and their knowledge that he knows what he's talking about. Or maybe they're going to choose to do something even better. Talk about a slap in the face! They're going to list it with this other guy at the same price — you know, the guy he just got done recommending. Sometimes they do that.

They call the new guy and say, "Can you give us a Broker's Price Opinion (BPO)? We have a property we're going to list with you." They do not tell him, thinking he's not going to know, that it's been in the MLS. He gets on the phone, calls the first broker who referred him, and says, "I just got a call from Fannie Mae. They want to list something with me. I think it's the property you had." He says, "Yes, it is. They want you to do a BPO. You had better go do it."

He goes and does his thing, then comes back to Fannie Mae and says, "You have to lower the price." They may even call a third agent to do a BPO. All these people are talking to each other. They all know it.

Now Fannie Mae finally decides that they're going to lower the price. They lower the price, and list it with this second agent. Both agents have already spoken. The first agent will tell the second agent, "I've got somebody who wants that deal. I've already seen his resume, cash in his bank, a letter from The Norris Group, and his history. As a matter of fact, he's already bought deals from me. He's a player. He's waiting."

Remember, when this property was originally listed, the second agent got the same response. None of his investors wanted it. When it was in the MLS, he called everyone as well. Typically what happens in this situation is the property gets a kind of stigma. They're a little worried about giving it to their favorite guys as it is. Now they have to convince some investor to take it while the investor is worried about dollars and cents.

When that property price is lowered, there's a very high probability that you're going to get the deal. The first agent will have already told the second agent, "Here's my guy." They both will share the commission. The only reason you're going to score that deal is because you went in there and talked to them. You showed them, and you won them over a little bit. Now it's a dog property at the right price. No one else wanted it. No one else wants it now, either. They don't even know what the price is. That property is going to make it to the MLS all right, but believe me, you are already in first place with a signed offer. That's it!

Now, for those of you who read more into what I just wrote in the past few pages, let me make it clear. Professional REO agents do not give their favorite investors an illegal or improper edge over anyone else. As a matter of fact, I lose more deals than I get. We do get calls right to our cell phones, and we do get a heads up on properties being put into the MLS sometimes even before they are listed. (I call this pre-listing favoritism.) However, that's as far as it goes.

We don't get access to the property any faster than anyone else. We are in line with everyone else to make our offers, and if there's a multiple offer situation we have NO edge. It typically goes to a highest and best offer situation. Where we do get an edge is on things that fall out of escrow. We get a call that puts us in first place about a deal that we might be interested in, but why is that? Because we have the ability to close that transaction immediately and without hesitation or contingencies of any kind. Usually on a pending deal falling out of escrow, the asset managers will favor closing the transaction on the original escrow closing date, and that requires cash (real cash – not hard-money loans) and someone who can move quickly without asking for contingencies and all that nonsense.

I want to tell you the truth about this because most hardworking real estate agents get unfairly suspected of this kind of stuff all of the time, and it is the biggest lie in the real estate business.

Many times, I have seen guys selling seminars on how to get an edge by handing an envelope full of cash to an REO agent. That's BS.

Everybody thinks top real estate agents play favorites with the investors they give deals to; that they hold back offers and only submit the offers they want, for whomever they want, while the rest get thrown in the trash. This is more BS! Nothing could be further from the truth.

Yes, it's true that these agents love doing business with responsible professional investors and speculators that never let them down, that follow through and keep their commitments, but you have to understand that these guys will not under any circumstance run the risk of losing their multimillion-dollar accounts with the banks they work with for an additional few thousand dollars in commission (and that's if they are representing both sides of the transaction). Please! If they did, here is what they'd have to look forward to.

As I have told you, they have families, they are well-known in their communities, and they are well aware that if they did anything so stupid and irresponsible as to violate their own ethics, integrity and their fiduciary obligation to their multimillion-dollar clients, they could well lose their license, see all of their business disappear, destroy their lives and those of their loved ones within their communities, and quite frankly end up in jail. And all this just to sneak you a deal because why? How quickly would you do something that stupid for a few bucks?

These people build their lives and careers just like doctors, attorneys or any other professional, and that's why I (and many others) grow to love doing business with them. They are fair, decent people. They just happen to have chosen real estate as their profession.

Now I know every once in awhile you will read or hear on the news about some group of supposed real estate "professionals" getting arrested for doing exactly the same thing I just said is a lie. But please keep one thing in mind; those people getting arrested are not professional career real estate agents and brokers. They are professional crooks, temporarily pretending and posing as real estate professionals.

Today they're in real estate. Tomorrow they're running for public office and selling gun permits to their supporters or embezzling from some investment or finance company they talked into hiring them. These are just people without character that visit the real estate profession just like they do any other and get caught doing what comes natural to them personally. That is known as a character flaw, not endemic to any business or career.

So do your business with integrity, and do not expect compromising behavior from professionals that live and work right in the communities they serve. If you happen to accidently bump into one of these posers in the course of doing business, do yourself a favor and run like your life depends on it. Because I assure you, your freedom will.

Of all the professional real estate agents I have worked with over the years, the one agent that comes to mind as the best example of a professional, who clearly demonstrates all of the character attributes I have identified, is none other than my good and trusted friend Don Anderson of Prudential Troth Realtors of the Antelope Valley. He not only helped me to understand what is required of me to become a successful professional investor working with REO agents, but he taught me a few things about becoming a better man. He is a wonderful example of a dedicated and committed business leader and employer, a good and loving husband, a wonderful and considerate father, and one of my best friends.

Thank you, Don, for teaching me to be the best investor I could hope to be.

Tony Alvarez and Don Anderson

CHAPTER 17

Behind the Scenes

I want you to know one thing. I want to inject something here. When this market starts going haywire again with foreclosures, Fannie Mae may change the rules slightly. They might force these guys, as they were doing toward the end of the last downturn, to put all listings in the MLS for a certain amount of time. They might require the properties to be listed in the MLS for some minimum amount of time before they accept any offers at all. That just ruined my whole plan, or did it?

Why didn't it ruin my plan? You have the listing agent who had it first. He's a friend of the second agent who now has the listing, and he's obligated. The truth of the matter is a property that was $200,000 is now going to be listed for $175,000 or $150,000.

You're in the first position, even if they have to wait for offers. These agents, unlike representing a homeowner, have the right to call this guy from Fannie Mae and say, "We have 72 offers here. They're all higher than this one guy's offer." Your offer was $150,000 and everybody else's was $175,000. They're going to say, "We suggest you seriously consider taking this low offer. This is the offer you should really consider. This guy is a closer. We have worked with him before. It's solid!"

In most cases, they have to submit all of the offers. Some agents have flexibility with some of this stuff. Sometimes they just shut off, meaning they stop taking offers by a certain deadline. That's what happens. They can shut it off. They're going to get 20 offers on a property, and you were the first man in. Everyone else is saying, "Wait! I see it dropped. Now I'm going to come in there and redo my offer." Sometimes those offers don't even come in.

Another option they have to liquidate the property is instead of relisting as new, they would drop the original listing price, but they wouldn't put it in as a brand-new listing, just reduced. Honestly, what they do or how was never any of my concern. I'm only concerned with my performance.

Getting in there and developing that relationship is what gets you the call. When that listing comes back at a lower price, they're going to call you first. Now you've gone from last man on the totem pole with a dog property to the top of the heap. I hope you get this. It's gold!

Remember, if you pay too much for that dog property, you've lost the agent's respect. He's going to think you don't know what you're doing. I don't know about any other area in real estate. Maybe when you're buying something that's in nice shape or that's a nicer home, when you're competing with people, that's a different thing.

In this case, they look at your skills. If you don't know how to buy, at some point, you'll wake up and realize it. You're going to be in the middle of an escrow, and you'll call them and say, "I can't close." Now he has to go back to Fannie Mae and say, "I made a mistake. I'm an idiot." The 28-year-old Fannie Mae rep, who probably doesn't own his own house, will look bad. Remember, this is a web of contacts and connections that's a lot like dominos, all lined up next to each other. Hit one and they all could tumble.

CHAPTER 18

Love Your Agents

Since we know agents already have many investors to work with, you must answer the all-important question, why would they work with you? What do you bring to the table? These are the subtle changes that make a monumental difference.

Here comes that four-letter word: Love your agents.

I don't do a lot of quotes, but this is probably the best definition of what love is in this business I have ever heard. Memorize it, write it down, and read it every day before you start working, especially when you go to see any agent. Love your agents.

"I don't necessarily have to like my players and associates, but as their leader I must love them. Love is loyalty. Love is teamwork. Love respects the dignity of the individual. This is the strength of any organization."

— Vince Lombardi

Did you ever fall in love? It's not always love at first sight. When I met my girlfriend and fell in love, I said, "I'm chubby, but I'm cool. Come on! You want some. Come on!" Oddly enough, she's into bigger guys.

Whether you understand it or not, somebody is leading these relationships. Go deeper by leading the relationship, winning their hearts and minds, getting the best deals, and getting in first position.

To get to the best deals and get called first, you must do two things consistently well:

First, you must make agents love the way you work. This is all about performance.

Second, you must make agents love you for who you are, and this is all about relationship building which we will cover later.

CHAPTER 19

Make Agents Love the Way You Work

How? Understand your agent's fears and eliminate them.

What are their fears?

You won't close escrow. That's simple. It scares them to death. That's the worst thing. A Fannie Mae agent or any REO agent representing lenders is not a regular agent. Those are huge accounts that represent millions of dollars in commissions to them.

If you don't know what you're doing, that could be disastrous for them. They assume the worst. They think we're all idiots.

I want you to know that I have felt that. I know what it is to walk in, have the guy look at me, and say, "Sure, I'm going to forget about my regular investor guys who I've been working with for years to put myself on the hook with you."

Litigation is a big one, especially these days. You're going to be buying a property that's as-is, where-is, and with all the faults and defects. If you don't know what you're doing, you may come back to him and say, "Hey, I didn't know it had asbestos! I didn't know what that was. I didn't know the guy had dropped oil on his driveway and that it's considered toxic waste today."

You're inexperienced. You have no money or credit. The money side is not as important, but having proof that you have access to those funds is the same as if you have it in your pocket. They don't care where it comes from. These agents understand that you're going to have to come up with cash to buy this deal. It's a given. Some agents are more sensitive than others when it comes to this subject of cash offers, so beware. Understand how your agents think.

If you've ever bought an investment property using a hard-money lender and equity partners, you know you personally don't need either money or credit. How did I get started? You could have wrapped my credit report around this book twice. It was a disaster. I had no money except $6,000 that I borrowed from my dad, which was to pay for my own pizza.

Another major fear is that they will lose the account with the lender. You will make them look bad. Their reputation is everything to them.

It's all performance driven. Understand your agent's needs and wants. Know what the agent expects from you, and give it to them. Performance is everything. It requires speed and accuracy, so act fast. For everything having to do with the performance side of the business, move and don't hesitate. Don't let the fears in your mind stop you from getting the deal.

Trust, knowledge, experience, ability to perform, and loyalty sum it up. That's what he needs from you for him to want to pick up the phone and call you first every time. These things will come up over and over again, and you will realize that the only prerequisite you need once you understand the performance side of the business is the relationship-building side, which we will cover next. However, if you miss any of the five performance prerequisites, as the umpire says, "You're outta the game."

Do what you say you'll do, or don't say it.

I close fast. They know it will be a smooth transaction. I'm an agreeable buyer. I'm pleasant to deal with. I'm telling you, they love me. I'm a nice guy. My favorite question is, "What do you want me to do? What can I do to make it move more smoothly for you?"

By the way, this is crucial. Don't you dare walk into an agent's office to talk to him about buying deals if you're unsure about where you want to go or what you want to do. That's suicide. That's not what you want. You have to have a good sense of what you want to accomplish. You have to have a good sense of your numbers and be knowledgeable about your particular market.

Move quickly. Have cash or a lender in place for acquisitions. Understand repair costs accurately. Feel confident about your ability. If you walk into a professional agent's office and start coming off unsure about what your decisions will be or whether you can handle it, you're dead. He'll smell that on you like a bloodhound.

That's why it's so important to make a real and deep commitment right up front, to always be honest and tell them the truth about you, your level of knowledge, experience, money, everything. This falls under the category of do the right thing, regardless of the consequences.

Making a deep commitment to telling them the truth and not lying about anything will get rid of your false pretense and nervousness faster than anything you could ever imagine. Remember to be pleasant and honest. Show them you have integrity from the initial contact. Regardless of what your mind tells you, I promise you, over time, you will never regret it.

Tony Alvarez and Mic Blackwell

CHAPTER 20

Train Your Agents

Train your agents to understand what you want to buy. This will increase purchases and reduce rejections because you do not want to say no to them too many times. If you do, then you're history!

Have you ever tried dating someone new? You say, "Do you want to go out tonight?" They say "No, I'm busy. I have to do my hair." "What about Friday?" "No, I have to take care of my sister's kid." "What about next year?" "No, I think I'm going to be in Iraq." Will you be asking them out again? I don't think so. You'll be shredding their number and forgetting they exist. It's no different in business. You want to increase the times you say yes to that person because that will build up their confidence in dealing with you.

List properties for sale with the agent that originally sold you the deal, even if they are retired or dead. Are you getting my point? If they are dead, go back to that office and try to find out who they would want you to have it listed with. It's a silly thing, but it's important for me. I have had transactions where I've gone back to list the house with an agent and they're no longer an agent.

This is a courtesy that you should extend to any agent with whom you want to develop a long-term relationship. It's a sign of respect, and it's only common sense. Put yourself in their place.

There is an exception to this rule: Sometimes top listing agents are so busy with their listing clients that they actually consider it a burden to handle retail listings for their investor clients. In this case, ask them for a referral to list the property. Ask for their favorite buyer's agent or seller's agent. They will probably refer you to their best friend.

I list all my stuff with the agent who originally gave me the deal. I remember who gave me the deal when I first got started. I wasn't only buying from these three top REO agents. I was also buying from other agents as well. Some of them were first-time agents. They were the newbie agents, and many times they got me good deals. They are hungry, so they work harder than most.

I went back to visit an agent who had given me a deal once after a few years had passed. They said, "Phyllis doesn't work here anymore." I asked if we could call her at home. When I finally reached her, I said, "Phyllis, this is Tony. Remember me?" "Oh yes," she said. "Phyllis, remember that I told you I'd come back to list the property with you? Well, I'm back."

This is a house I bought for $40,000 that I'm now selling for $275,000. She's at home watching television. She's an older lady, and she gets the commission. She said, "I'm no longer an agent. What do we do?" I said, "Call somebody you like. Have them throw you a couple bucks." She lit up her license just for that deal. I like doing that kind of thing. Yes, it makes me feel good, but pay attention. Everyone in her office was watching. Now I'm a hero, and they all talk. How often do you get to witness a great, kind moment that shows you evidence of the best that we are capable of doing? It's no wonder I'm loaded. If I make money, you make money. Everybody's happy. WAKE UP!

Do yourself a huge favor. Stop reading this book right now. Go get on the internet and Google random acts of kindness and their effects on serotonin levels in the human brain. You will never see things the same again.

That's just my thing. It builds credibility when these agents know that you're coming back to them. It's part of the payoff. Not only that, but the other 50 agents in the office that watched me do that are now curious about working with someone who would care that much about their relationship with their agent. How tough do you think it is to get them to call me with their deals?

I am listing 30 properties within the next 45 days with the REO agent who had the most to do with making me wealthy. Is that nice? The average sales price will be $250,000. That's a nice paycheck. Remember that agents get a 6% commission. It's a strong motivation to control both sides of the deal. That's obvious.

Note:

When buying and structuring your offers, if you're new and just starting out in the business, larger deposits may help your offers to be taken more seriously. Of course, that's if you have money and feel confident about your offer. However, once you develop the relationship, it won't matter.

Special Benefit:

Once in awhile, I would get a call from some of the agents I had close relationships with, and they'd tell me they had a listing coming that they thought I'd be interested in. Sometimes I'd be out of town and not available to sign contracts. In those special cases, they signed for me to make sure I got the deal. Now, that's relationship building! I've only been able to accomplish that with a couple of my best agents. Other agents were too concerned about liability. I tell you this so you can see to what extent relationship building can help you reach your financial goals.

Now, let's get going. We are about to enter the best part of doing business; relationship building. Here is where you get to make friends with people who will love making you wealthy as you help do the same for them. This one element is actually part of the natural law, what is naturally a part of us as human beings and very much responsible for the reason our country became so prosperous so quickly.

SECTION I: PART 2

RELATIONSHIP BUILDING

"Your family and your love must be cultivated like a garden. Time, effort, and imagination must be summoned constantly to keep any relationship flourishing and growing."

- Jim Rohn

CHAPTER 21

Make Your Agents Love You for Who You Are

Abraham Lincoln had to motivate people to go to war. Talk about having to be persuasive! Come with me. We could die, but we'll have a lot of fun.

Abraham Lincoln once said,

"When the conduct of men is designed to be influenced, persuasion, kind, unassuming persuasion,should ever be adopted. It is an old and true maxim that 'a drop of honey catches more flies than a gallon of gall.' So with men. If you would win a man to your cause, first convince him that you are a sincere friend. Therein lies the drop of honey that catches his heart, which, say what he will, is the great high road to his reason and which, once gained, you will find but little trouble in convincing him of the justice of your cause if indeed that cause be a just one. On the contrary, assume to dictate to his judgment or to command his action and he will retreat within himself, close all avenues to his heart and head. Such is man, and so must he be understood by those who would lead him."

What does that whole thing say besides to be nice to people? Treat them with respect and dignity, and they will love you until the day they die.

Let them know you're going to do a good job and that you're really interested in their well-being FIRST! You're a closer, and you're going to make it happen. This is relationship building. It's not about performance.

Developing solid, long-term business relationships requires time and patience. Slow down and listen. The performance side requires speed. Slow down for relationships. For example, let's say you want to make friends with someone. Do you run up to them like you're jacked up on caffeine and rattle off the following? "Let's be friends. Come on. Hurry up! You want to come over? Huh? Huh? Huh?" That's not going to work. "Hey, let's get together in your office. Come on! I have something to do. Hurry up! Let's look at the plaques. Oh yeah, that's nice. That's nice. That's nice. I don't know anything about that one. Give me a deal. I took the seminar. I know all about you, or I will. I love you...."

I have a favorite episode of *Everybody Loves Raymond*. This is a personal thing at our house. It's a big joke. I run home to watch that show every night. It's my family. If you ever see that show, that's my mom and dad.

Ray's wife is going through her time of the month, and he's trying to be helpful. He read something somewhere and he knows what to do. He runs to the store and gets her all kinds of stuff. He comes home and says, "Here, honey. You don't have to suffer this month." He's worried about himself so he wants to drug her up. She sees through his selfish motive and screams, "I can't believe it! You don't understand me!" She goes on for 10 minutes. "You idiot! Don't you realize...?"

Just as she's telling Raymond, "I hate you!" the phone rings and she picks up the phone with a very polite voice, saying, "Hello. Yes, Mary. How are you?" She starts laughing. Talk about a paradigm shift! He's standing there with his mouth open, and she has just abused him to heck. "All right. We'll see you tomorrow. Bye. Oh, gosh, she's so nice." He says, "Can we get her on speed dial?" She starts up again and says, "That's why you're such an idiot! You don't understand that all I need is to be hugged. I want to feel loved. When I feel like this, I just want to be hugged!" So he jumps up and throws his arms around her and she shrieks, "What are you doing?" "You said you want to be hugged." "Not now, you idiot!"

We're talking timing. Don't walk in there saying, "I'm going to love you, but I want my $10 million at the end of it."

Start to think about your business relationships as friends. Do not keep them an arm's length apart from you. They're not an attorney. They're not looking to cause you harm. It's your responsibility to get beyond that hurdle in your own mind. It's a fear. You need to understand yourself a little bit and root that out.

That's why I got the $7.2 million and those other investors didn't. They're still working on an old paradigm. I started using the word "love" a lot and thought, "Geez! I'm starting to sound like Leo Buscaglia. Remember him, the liberal love guy?"

I have my own political views, and I want you to know that it's not Democrat or Republican. I grew up in Massachusetts where we prayed to the Kennedys every morning, but I also come from Cuba where I know what it is to be in the receiving side of Communism and Socialistic policies. I have my own views. I am more conservative, and I am, in some areas, very liberal. I love people. I don't know you at all, but I have a tremendous affection for you. And I care about you doing well financially. I understand that at a deep level we are all connected, and we need to help each other do well financially and live full lives.

Be Grateful:

Remember to be grateful. I can't tell you this enough. It's a small thing, but that one thing will put you ahead of the pack. The majority of investors don't stop to say thank you. Recognize the agents' importance to your success, and show them. This is key. It's a simple statement.

If you have kids, don't you tell them that you love them on their birthday? Do you not say Happy Birthday? Don't you buy them a card? If you really love someone, don't you look forward to doing something for them? These people are going to make you rich. You'd better love them to death. Take to slobbering all over them. Be generous to them.

Treat these people like you would want to be treated. That's not a big hurdle unless your self-esteem is down by the carpet somewhere.

Stay in touch. Remember to keep yourself in their minds at all times. Do whatever you can to be paramount in their mind.

I have a family member and although we don't agree on a lot of things, I admire him for one trait. He has been a sales guy all his life, but it took him many years to figure out how to hold on to his success. He always did half the job extremely well, the performance side.

In my opinion, the part he does well is he stays in touch with people. He knows how to do that. His first task in the morning is to call potential clients. Even if he's not doing business with you right now, he tries to find a way to make that connection, and he's relentless. The only problem is his calls are only motivated by the bottom line.

If your business relationships are strictly about business, they won't have any lasting power because there's not a common thread to hold them beyond the dollars. The initial sale is as close as you'll ever get.

Bill Tan & Tony Alvarez - IRCA Meeting

CHAPTER 22

Hey, Call Me! Let's Do Lunch

I hear the lunch thing thrown around a lot. I have made $7.2 million in seven years. I've been out there doing real estate deals since 1980, and I have never done lunch with anybody. I've never had one lunch with any of these guys, and I like to eat. They offer all the time. Out of those three agents, there's only one who is a lunch guy. He has been calling me for years. "Come on, Tony! Let's get lunch." It's just not my thing. I don't break my workday in the middle to go have lunch.

On the other hand, my good friend Mike Cantu, another successful Southern California real estate investor who I adore, said he has lunch three or four times a week with friends and business people. That's his thing. I don't do lunches. Heaven only knows how much money I've passed up because I don't do them. That will be something you can figure out.

As you can see, relationship building is different for everyone. It's doesn't matter if you do lunch or don't do lunch. Do whatever works for you. The bottom line is that you do something that goes beyond the deal. That's the point I want you to take away. And don't be afraid to love people and truly care about them first. Live your life completely.

Jack Fullerton, Tony Alvarez and Mike Cantu
Millionaire Maker Seminar

CHAPTER 23

Contact and Communication

Contact and communication is paramount. I already made that obvious. Now let's take your business relationship to a deeper level. Is that possible without having sex? I don't know.

Understand what is important to them personally. We kind of touched on that. The plaques and all that are deep, but let's go a little deeper. Know their personal likes, like cruises, foods, snowmobiles and RVs. Do you think I'm kidding you? I am not. If this guy makes me $7.2 million, do you think I'm going to flinch on buying him a cruise if I know that's what his wife and him love?

The first time I walked into one of my top REO agent's offices, I saw a picture on his wall where he and his wife were standing behind one of those big wooden steering wheels on a cruise ship. When you go on a cruise, before you board, they make you take a stupid picture of you standing next to the steering wheel in hopes you will buy it later. It's a touristy thing. I saw that picture on his wall and asked him, "Do you do cruises? I would love to do a cruise, but I don't know what to do." Well, he went on for over an hour telling me everything you could possibly want to know about cruises and how to save money and how to get the best rooms, which ones to go on, which ones to avoid, and on and on and on. It seems he and his wife go on cruises four or five times a year. They're certified cruise-a-holics trying to get through their 12-step program.

I used every tip he gave me, and it worked. I took my mother on a cruise to Mexico. We got a great room with a full balcony for half the price. Isn't that cool? We had a great time. I enjoyed every minute of my cruise and every second of my conversation with the agent. And were we talking business? No. But were we building our relationship? You betcha! Are you getting this?

Now, you know I'm going to do business with this guy. He made me $7.2 million, and he taught me how to get a great cruise for half the price. We've had endless conversations about everything under the sun. I know the cruises he has done and the ones he hasn't done, but is looking forward to doing.

I bought him a gift certificate. You can call any cruise line. You don't have to buy the actual cruise, but you can buy a gift certificate they can use toward anything they want to do. Do you think that maybe he was appreciative of that when he got it? He realized that I listened to him. I realized what's important to him and his wife. I took hard-earned dollars, which, by the way, he put into my pocket. I didn't bribe him. I didn't say, "Meet me tomorrow. I have $2,000 in cash in an envelope just to say thanks."

There will be some agents who will say, "I want to ride with you," but they don't want to be your partners. They don't want the liability. They just want part of your profit. If you lower your standards and do that, they will write you off. You can love these people, and you don't have to bribe them. You don't have to lower your integrity or standards one bit.

I was having a conversation with Rick Solis, who's a good friend, appraiser and very successful real estate investor in Southern California (my background is also as an appraiser). We were talking about the appraisal business. I was telling him that one of the things I love about what I do is I don't experience burnout. If you can work at any business where you can conduct yourself with integrity and you respect what you do, it has a weird affect on your life.

Can you tell me another job that has that benefit? I'm a Catholic, and I don't even think priests are up there anymore. I'm having a problem with that because if you think about it, appraisers are always under a lot of pressure from everybody in the transaction, such as the person who's buying or selling or the lender, no wonder there's such a high percentage of burn out in the appraisal business.

It's wonderful to be in a business the way I do it where I love what I do. I love the people, and I can conduct myself with self-respect and dignity, and there's no end to it.

Mike Cantu and Tony Alvarez

CHAPTER 24

Make it Personal

Any chance you get, every time you can, proactively take your business relationships to a deeper level. Do your best to understand what is important to them personally more and more. Get to know their personal likes and dislikes as if they were your own.

I want you to also catch the subtle changes. You can't just meet an agent today, talk about his listings, and then next week send him a gift certificate. You don't know the guy. That's not appropriate, and it's not going to work. This is a series of slow, simple steps. None of them are complicated.

Know their families, children, schools, fundraisers, etc. I've covered that somewhat, and I can't drill it home enough. Know what they value. Know which charities, clubs and sports teams they support.

I'm not a sports guy. I saw a movie one time. It was a war movie where Americans capture an American soldier, thinking he's the enemy because he's disguised himself in a Nazi uniform in order to get safely back to the allied troops. So now they are interrogating him with a gun to his head asking, "Who won the World

Series in 1935?" That's how they were going to prove that he was really not a spy. My brains would be on the floor because there's no way I'm going to know the answer to that question.

You'll run into guys who live and die by sports. If you don't know anything about sports and you get a chance to open up a conversation, make your question, "I'm not a sports guy. What is it that fascinates you about that? I've never understood it."

If he's a sports nut, like a football guy or a basketball guy, you'd better have some time because he's going to tell you everything. When you leave there, you'll say, "I wish I never would have asked. I'm going to kill Alvarez for that one!"

Familiarity removes doubt and creates confidence! If there's one statement of mine that I would say for you to write down and remember, that would be it. That really puts it in a nutshell for us.

The more you can create that link between you and them, the better off you're going to be.

Make them remember you with a smile. Don't ever leave the office of an agent who could make you wealthy with them feeling awkward, angry or disappointed. Any negative emotion you leave him with, that's the first thing he's going to remember when he sees you again. Leave him with a smile.

CHAPTER 25

Be Prepared to Go Deeper

Maybe the relationship starts and then something goes awry. This happened to me with the agent who's given me the majority of my business. Sometimes he can be a hard butt. His personality is such that he can be difficult to deal with at times. I honestly believe we've succeeded because I've worked at understanding his personality traits.

We've worked together very well because I've really worked hard at winning him over, and not dishonestly. I saw things in his character that I really liked. I knew there was a human being in there somewhere. I just had to find him.

I had a situation with him where we butted heads when he was upset. He can be really rude. I think it concerned some of the listings we had. I can't remember exactly right now, but the gist of it is that the reason for it wasn't as important as the fact that we were diametrically opposed. He was very convinced that he was right, and I was very convinced that he wasn't.

Isn't it funny? I can't remember the reason. I can just remember his anger. I went in to talk to him and I was really upset. I was totally focused on letting this guy know that he was wrong. He was trying to let me know that I was wrong. He was doing it sarcastically, which is his way. He's very good at that. He can be very abusive without knowing it. I don't believe we consciously decide to hurt people.

Somewhere along the line when I was letting him go at me, I realized that he was not talking to me. Some of the things he threw at me had nothing to do with our problem. I calmed down and let him go.

When it was all done, I kept quiet. I said, "When I came in here, I was really angry at you over this. You said a lot of things to me that ripped through me, but I'm not going to respond about this to you. The only thing I'm thinking about right now is that we're really good friends. You've done a lot of stuff for me that nobody else would do, so I have no problem forgiving you for making me feel the way you just made me feel."

This was a conversation with a broker who owns 50% of his office. That's kind of an intimate response. We're talking about feelings here. I feel like Richard Simmons. Do you remember him? He hugged everybody.

I was really hurt at the way he was speaking to me but when I left, he was calmed down. I went back a couple of days later. He called me into his office and we sat down. He said, "Before we talk about anything, I have to get something off my chest." Then I was scared because I was thinking, "This guy is going to fire me as an investor. He can't live with looking at me because it reminds him of that whole scene."

He said, "I need to tell you a story." He went on to tell me a story about his relationship with his dad, the man that he hates, and how his father belittled him his whole life. I don't want to belittle that conversation, but I don't think it's necessary for me to go into the details. In the middle of it, his eyes welled up with tears. By the way, that's not the first or last time that teary-eyed situation occurred during the years I've worked with him. Just for the record, I also had a similar dad who I love very much.

While I was learning all those things about him, it also taught me that maybe while I was so focused on his anger and all the things he was saying to me that had nothing to do with us doing business, I was reacting to him with the same anger because we locked horns about exactly the same thing.

I had the same problems with my dad that this guy had with his dad. Somehow, we were doing deals and yelling at each other over something that had nothing to do with business. I expressed to him my situation with my dad. He talked to me about his dad, and we left. Now, did we leave a little bit tighter than the day before? Did we get a little bit closer to being like brothers than business people? Yes, we did! These are the true reasons why he and I are such close friends today. This is the stuff that deep-rooted, trusted business friendships are forged over. NOT the deal!

CHAPTER 26

Lighten Up

Make them remember you with a smile.

I use humor. I make them remember me as the most pleasant moment in their otherwise stress-filled day. A lot of them hate their jobs. If you can, become Dr. Laura, a therapist, a shoulder. Honestly, look to become close friends.

I'll wear a dress for $7.2 million. I mean that. I become the person they talk to about an otherwise really rude investor. I become their break from work. I make them laugh. They always smile when they see me. I sincerely love this, folks. And I want nothing, but to make their lives heaven.

That's the one thing I always remember. If they don't smile when they see me, I know I have a problem. I poke fun at myself and our business. I do that a lot. I really think that for all the ins and outs of it, we're all blessed.

I ask about them and their families first. I don't walk in there talking about a deal, even if we've already developed a relationship. Even if I'm brand-new, I never ask about the deal first. Don't ever do that. What's the point? That tells them exactly what you're about.

If you are going in there talking about the deal first, it's going to be a hard deal and you will never see the top spot on their list. I become their friend. That's all. I become the person they complain to about some rude investor.

CHAPTER 27

Timing is Everything

I'm going to tell you a short story. I went into this guy's office again. As you can tell, I go where the fish are. I asked the girl in the front office (who was on the phone), "Is he in?" She whispered, "Yes, he's on the phone," smiled and pointed her fingers towards his office. That means to go on in. Since she leaves the desk a lot, our thing is that if she gets called on doing that for me, she says, "I didn't see him come in. How'd he get in there?" and I play along.

I went into his office. He was on the phone. He looked up and saw me. He pointed to the chair that means "sit down until I'm done." I sat down and he said, "Yes. I understand." He hung up the phone and sighed. He was pale. He looked like he just got some bad news, like someone in his family died. God forbid one of his children had a car accident or something.

I didn't know what to do because that's an awkward moment. I said the most honest thing I could say to him. "What's wrong?" I asked. He looked at me and said, "Sometimes I wonder what the heck I'm doing in this business and why I deal with investors."

Do you remember when I was in Lawrence, Massachusetts and the kids used to tell me, "Those damn Cubans are moving in," and I used to say, "You're right. They're taking over!" Then without missing a beat, I said, "You're right. Those damn investors!"

He said, "Tony, do you know so-and-so?" He mentioned some investor. He was the same investor I taught how to do the Section 8 program in my area. He's a big guy. He has a lot of bucks. This agent was also feeding him deals. He was doing it for years before he met me. The guy is filthy rich. He's beyond rich. It's beyond ludicrous. This investor was out there long before I ever showed up.

He said, "I was just talking to him, and I've been feeding him some deals. The problem is that I haven't sold these last deals as fast as I have been in the past," because just like me, this investor chooses to relist properties with the agent who originally gave him the deal. That investor, who's a professional investor is worth about $30 million, is not small potatoes.

The agent continued and said, "He just called me to tell me that I didn't sell those listings fast enough, and by the way, he has some other houses he was going to list with me that he bought someplace else. He's just calling up to tell me no. He's going to give those listings to another agent in town, some young whippersnapper who has been selling stuff really quickly, because I didn't move them quickly enough."

You tell me. Is that not the dumbest thing that guy could've done? This man is feeding him deals. He's a Fannie Mae approved broker. I'll tell you why he did that. When real estate investors become rich and successful, they become egotistical. They think they're the only ones with a brain. They think they did it alone.

Do you know why I know investors get egotistical? It's because I've made all of those mistakes. I know what it is to be that idiotic.

I was standing there. He was hanging the phone up. He was wiped out emotionally. He said, "Do you know how many millions of dollars I've handed that guy?" I said, "Yes, I do." He said, "He called me up just to ruin my day." I said, "I can see that."

He said, "I have five deals coming that I had marked for him. I'm not giving him one." I said, "You shouldn't. He does not deserve your business because he doesn't understand what you go through." There was a long pause. Then, I broke the silence with, "You know... I think I'd be willing to buy those five deals. Would you sell them to me? Another long pause. "Please?"

Now, did I get those deals? You're damn right I did. And why? Because of timing. Don't forget this lesson. Remember this when you're wondering why you should even bother starting new relationships with these agents when they already have professional investors like me they've been dealing with for years. Even the best of romances periodically crash and burn. Your job is to be consistent about your efforts to reach out to those brokers and agents as often as possible. Timing is everything.

A year later, I got to talk to that investor. He called me and wanted to meet me. He knew I had started the Section 8 rental program, and he knew I did it successfully. I didn't have a lot of problems in my office because Section 8 tenants can sometimes be problematic if you don't have the systems in place to deal with them. I had done a good job.

He said, "A lot of people talked to me about what you did. Would you please take the time to tell me about it?" I got to meet him. We became very good friends, and I also got the opportunity to tell him, "Do you know why you lost that account? Do you know why I have it?"

I want you to know that this is the test, not only of an intelligent human being and a successful investor, but it's also a test of a wise man. That guy is one of my best buddies right now. He knows I took that account. He knows the same story you do. He's laughed with me the same way. That's why I know how to tell it.

I've sat in his office. His wife loves me to death. His son started working with him two years ago and is already a millionaire. He loves me because he's like you. He's that cut above the average investor. He didn't get mad at me. He learned from that situation.

Do you know that I am solely responsible for him picking up the phone, calling that agent up and apologizing, even though he never got the account back?

This man is an Israeli. He has an Israeli accent, which I love. He's wonderful. And I love the Israeli people. They're the salt of the earth, loving people, and have produced some of the most brilliant minds in history. In fact, if you knew what's been invented by that tiny little country, you'd fall over. Did you know that most high-tech companies have research divisions in Israel? From the cell phone in your pocket to the best weapons systems in the world, to the security system that we use at the airports, to the chips in our computers, all of them designed by the Israeli divisions of major high-tech corporations. They're amazing people, and I love them. Historically, they have been huge contributors to the advancement of both the standard and quality of life for everyone on the planet, and we owe them a tremendous debt.

Now is that amazing or what?

Later on, that investor called the agent and said, "I just spoke to Tony, and I realize what I did. I just want to call you and apologize because you don't deserve that." I suggested that he walk there and talk to the guy, but he didn't. He did it on the phone. It's a little thing, but I told you before that this is a web of contacts and connections.

I have done deals with that investor. I've bought from him. He's bought from me. He has 300 single-family homes in our area. He called me recently and said, "Do you think I ought to start selling?" I said, "I'll call you when I'm done listing mine." You can change the whole market with one decision.

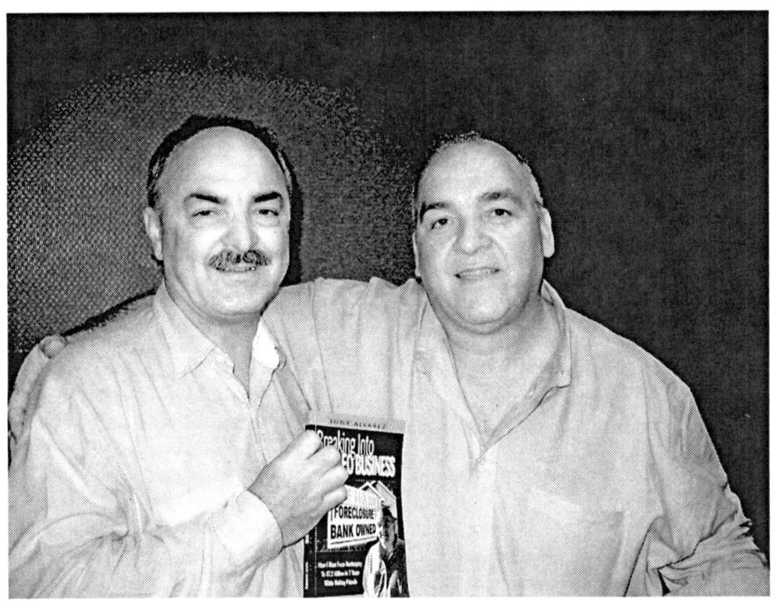

Miles Lipovich and Tony Alvarez

CHAPTER 28

Give Them Your Gratitude

Say thank you whenever possible, and do it in creative ways. Do it so everyone sees. I love nothing more than walking into that office and doing something for one of those agents that everyone in that office is going to know about it, because nobody does that.

Let's face it, broker/agent relationships are basically love/hate relationships. For example, one day I walked into an office where they had chocolates for sale at the front counter. I don't need a lot of push for that anyway. It was a fundraiser thing that the broker's daughter was doing.

I walked in there, looked and said, "Ooh, chocolates!" It happened to be the stuff I love. It was the bars with almonds. You can either get them with or without the almonds. I hate to give you so much information, but I have to be explicit about this in case one of you decides to send me chocolate – and please don't do it (almonds). My mom will kill you. She wants me to lose a little weight.

I walked in there. I went up to the counter being my nice, jovial self, and said, "Hi, how are you doing? What's going on? You have chocolates." She said, "Yes, the ones you like." I said, "Ooh, a fundraiser." She sighed and said, "Yes, another fundraiser."

She's been there a million and one years. I saw that. Why did she do that? She did that because they all resent the fact that the broker's kid brings in the chocolate, puts it on the front counter, and they feel obligated to buy it. It's a bar of chocolate. It's $2. It used to be $1. Inflation!

What do I do? I buy the whole box for a whopping $150. Woo-hoo! I'm going to suffer over that one, and I get to take all the chocolate and tell my mom and girlfriend I had to do it because it's a business thing.

When I said, "I'll buy it all," she looked at me and said, "Are you crazy?" I said, "Just give me the chocolate, will you?" She looked at me and smiled. She caught on right away. She said, "Oh, Tony." I said, "Let's do it."

I wrote a check. I'm really terrible at my personal finances. I have somebody else help me with that, so immediately when I did that, I thought, "I hope I have money in the bank. I hope I have enough funds to cover this check." I always worry about that when I make a good decision. I worry about whether it's going to happen or whether God is going to reach down and say, "Let's play with you for a little while."

I told her, "Would you do me a favor? Would you pass these out to the agents and tell them it's a gift from the broker?" It's a little thing. Do you know how many bars of chocolate those agents already bought? It isn't a trip to Hawaii. It's chocolate.

I went to talk to the broker. I sat in his office. "How are you doing? What's happening? How's the family?" We were talking for a while and then all of a sudden, one agent came in and said, "Hey, boss, thanks!" "Sure, we'll see you." "Bye." The broker didn't know what the heck was going on. We were talking a little bit more. Another guy came in and said, "I already bought 25 of these from you. I don't need another bar," and then he left.

After about the fourth person, the broker called up front and said, "Could you please have people stop coming in here? I'm talking to Tony." The girl said, "It's the chocolate thing," and she went on to tell him what I did. This was his daughter's fundraiser. He then looked up at me and his bottom lip started quivering and his eyes went glassy. He was emotional.

The reason why that happened like that is because I zeroed in on one fact. The people in his office resented the fact that he was bringing those candy bars into the office. He was aware of that, but he didn't want to say no to his daughter. I turned that around.

"Dad, can I put this in your office? I have to sell 300 boxes so I can go on a trip." He didn't want to say, "No, honey, you can't." He's the boss. His daughter is looking up to him. "Come on. You own the place. You mean you can't do this? Okay. I'm not going to be a broker!"

Did that get my harpoon in a little bit deeper? I hate to use that term, but it fits. Were we closer? Did he know that I understood his plight? That's really what happens in that moment. In that moment, when he looked at me and his eyes were welled up with tears, he saw that we were one. I understood him in that moment.

I knew just how to handle that, not so I would get all the agents in the office patting me on the back. I wasn't getting any deals from them. I only wanted him to know what I did. You people are going to be eating chocolate like you will not believe.

Tony Alvarez, Daniel "Rudy" Ruettiger, Mike Cantu, Jack Fullerton, Bruce Norris, Ben Gay III Millionaire Maker Seminar

CHAPTER 29

There's Never Been Another You

Now, I want you to wake up. Sit up and listen carefully to what I have to tell you. You MUST learn to find what is unique in you and use it. I already told you that I use humor. You don't have to go in there and dance like me. You don't have to do what I do. You can be pleasant. If you look in yourselves, you will find what is unique in you that you bring to the table, and that is your saving grace.

If you try to imitate me, you're going to flop. That's what makes my relationship with him mine. That's what protects your relationship with the same agent during the same market. That's what keeps your relationship yours.

In order for you to have a clear understanding of the point I'm trying to make, to know your intrinsic value as a human being, you must first understand the answer to this question.

Ask yourselves this question when, in this lifetime or any lifetime, has there ever been another you? Meaning, have you ever been duplicated? Even if you're a twin, you are unique in all respects. And so, your ability to connect with another human being on a personal level must be based on what is uniquely inherent in your own character. Even in the way you smile, apologize, or deliver a good morning. You must never overlook the fact that it is completely different than anyone else. I always refer to love relationships or personal relationships when trying to explain this uniqueness. Why is it that people fall in love with certain people and not others? Why do we find certain people attractive and not others? Joan Rivers, the comedian, said, "If only 10% of the population loves me and finds me worth watching, I'll be pretty well-off financially."

For many years, I went along doing my business as usual, just being the person I have always been and never questioning my own behavior… that is until I crashed and burned in the early 1990s and ended up in bankruptcy. I was astounded at my ability to work so hard and then lose everything as if none of it ever happened.

I promised myself that I would take my time and seek new knowledge, not only about the secrets (if there were any) of how to accumulate wealth, but also about how to hang on to it, which apparently was one of my biggest setbacks.

This search led me to discover the study of my own mind, and that exploration has never and will never end. One of the most fascinating things that confounded me for most of my real estate investing life was the difficulty in answering for myself the following simple question: Why would anyone choose to do business with me? Especially when in most cases I would go into real estate offices that had been in business for many years, and they already had been working with other investors for many years. I must admit I didn't understand it much beyond the obvious (like they sell houses and I buy them.) Then one day, I was sitting at home flipping through the channels and I landed on PBS; one of my favorite channels simply because most of the time they have great stuff. This day was no different. Dr. Wayne Dyer was doing a presentation on his book called The Power of Intention (great book, by the way.) Anyway, he goes on to explain how an act of kindness can literally alter the serotonin levels in the brain, and how this can have a huge effect on us without even our approval. It just happens naturally.

Below is a clear explanation of this from the website www.GiftofKindness.com.

> "Serotonin is a chemical in the brain that is related to feeling good. Research shows that being on the receiving end of an act of kindness actually increases your serotonin levels substantially thus giving you a natural boost of the 'feel goods.' The great news about giving the gift of kindness to someone is that it's not only the receiver who benefits but also the person who delivers the act of kindness, almost equally. And it doesn't stop there. Anyone who witnesses the act or later hears about it also benefits from elevated levels of serotonin."

WOW! That was huge! I mean, can you imagine that? All at once, it hit me. That's all I had been doing! Everything from treating people with respect and dignity, to choosing to tell them the truth of any situation regardless of the consequences, to buying a few chocolates to support a young child's church or softball team (chocolates, by the way, that I loved to eat and couldn't wait to stuff in my mouth.) All of it. EVERY SINGLE ACT had been interpreted as an act of kindness, and ultimately created a bond between myself and people I had met as complete strangers that had grown to love me and I them.

What a wake-up call!

Could this be possible? Could it really be that simple? I am here to tell you that yes, it is that simple.

There are no magic pills for creating long-term success in business, or anywhere else for that matter. Business relationships (business friendships, if you will) are forged by truly caring for the other person's success as much as your own.

By honestly helping them to achieve their goals along the way as you achieve yours, and serving as a coach of sorts for each other, a supporter in our stress-filled times and a cheering section in our times of success and happiness.

By thanking them for all they do for you throughout the year, even if it's not a holiday, and recognizing they also value and want to experience the freedom you love and pursue for yourself and your family. At the core, believe me; we are all in the pursuit of the same dream. We just imagine it differently as individuals.

You may learn strategies and techniques that you can use for making deals and negotiating and they will help you to make money, but only being pleasant, kind and caring in all your business affairs will lead you to finding a place in your life full of peace and true, lasting wealth.

I don't want to get religious on you, but I believe in God. I believe things are set up in a certain way, and if you follow the rules, they work. That's why it works. I don't think God really cares about the performance side, but I assume He does care about our conduct. There is no other explanation for me reaching this level of financial success. NONE!

As I previously mentioned, if you conduct yourself with the utmost integrity and strive for that, and you catch yourself when you make mistakes and you turn them around, I think you'll get further ahead.

Tiffany Humfeld, Tony Alvarez, and Kyle Humfeld

CHAPTER 30

Appreciate Your Agents

Write letters of appreciation to their superiors. If they're not the broker in the office, write a letter to somebody they have to answer to and say thanks. "That guy or young lady in your office is wonderful. I'm an investor. I'm going to stick with them because they're honest and sincere." No other investor will. I promise you.

Be honest. How many of you ever send a thank-you letter to an agent you work with? Write letters of appreciation to their superiors, because no other investor will. Our words and actions wield tremendous power and set a tone for who we are, not them.

You're building yourself. You're building the foundation for you. Your actions say nothing about anyone else.

Remember what we have learned about an act of kindness and its effect on our serotonin levels. This was created in us purposely without our approval or concern. Do not ignore or overlook these truths. They will change not only how you do business and your results, but who you decide to be, your entire life experience.

CHAPTER 31

Advantages of Working With Agents

Advantage 1: They're deal machines.

They have constant incoming deals. Why? Because professional REO brokers typically specialize in handling distressed properties and distressed situations. That means when the REO inventory dries up, they will get the probates, divorce cases, illnesses, job losses, corporate transfers, fire-damaged houses, everything and anything that can cause someone to lose their home or become a desperate seller. These listings usually end up on their desks because everyone recommends these agents as the "go to" people when you want to get rid of your property quickly.

I use them because I'm lazy. I want to put in a small effort and over time, end up with a huge result that lasts forever. Can you imagine if I started working out? I'd have to find that steroid pill you take to grow muscles.

Advantage 2: There's no negotiating.

If you go into this business, you'll find that none of that negotiation stuff is any good. You need to make friends instead.

This stuff cracks me up. I get to go around making friends, and they bring me millions of dollars in deals. I don't have to butt heads with anybody. I don't have to find your button to push it so you say yes to me.

Multiple times a week, I'm reaching out to different brokers and agents and the only thing I'm asking them to do is to call me with some dog property that they need to get rid of anyway. How tough is that?

And remember: The deal they're going to call you with the first time, the one that's going to make you shine, is the one nobody wanted, so who are you competing with? I wish I knew this stuff before I got started. It was so simple, and I was making it so hard.

Advantage 3: There's no searching for sellers. The agent does it.

Advantage 4: You only need one good run.

I can quit today and if I never do anything else again, I'm okay. If I sell everything, I can sit back by that pool. The pool thing is boring now, though. That's why I'm here. You fall in love with this part of the business because it doesn't have the burnout at the end.

Advantage 5: You can train your agent to know what it is that you want.

This will save you time and increase the number of purchases you make.

Advantage 6: With the right relationship, you can even have your agents sign your offers for you.

Advantage 7: These agents don't mind you approaching other agents.

They understand they can only require your loyalty on listings they control themselves. They can't ask you to be loyal on inventory they don't control, like another agent's listing. You can't do it, either. Try calling Domino's Pizza and asking them to send you over a bucket of Kentucky Fried Chicken. It ain't gonna work. They can only send you what's in their control. Get it?

In other words, you aren't working with these REO brokers as an exclusive buyer's agent; you are developing individual relationships with individual REO broker agents. Over time, this will yield the highest return for your efforts and have a positive exponential effect on your business success.

CHAPTER 32

Disadvantages of Working with Agents

Disadvantage 1: Training your agent is time-consuming

You must spend time with the agents so they'll deliver you what you want. The reason for that is because you don't want to say no to them a lot of times. If you say no to them one too many times, you're history. And it doesn't matter if you can justify everything.

If you can justify the first time, you're okay. After the second or third time, goodbye. That's telling them that you don't know what you're doing or that you're too afraid to make a decision.

Disadvantage 2: One mistake and you're out.

If you make one mistake, not two, you run the risk of losing the agent, and you'll lose a great part of your business. I told you, I get 70% from one guy. If we didn't love each other, I'd have a hard time sleeping. If he walks on me, I have to start brand-new and start looking for a new agent. One way to minimize this potential headache is to be constantly in the market introducing yourself to new agents. Make it part of your business plan to meet every single agent that's registered in your Multiple Listing Service. In our office, that is exactly our goal every year. That's our goal. It has to be.

If you're going to do this business, make it part of your plan to do it all the way. Why do it halfway?

Disadvantage 3: You can't afford an "off" day.

I have a lot of off days. I get cranky, probably because I don't have enough to do. But you can't afford an off day. If you have one off day, you're risking a large part of your business. You can't have one. If you're a person who's moody, find a way to handle it. Get it out of your day, and do not show it to these agents.

As you develop your relationships with these guys and they become friends, this opens the door for you to express things to them. In all honesty, the only times I've ever found myself confiding in them about my life or things that bother me are when they've opened the door and told me something personal. That helps me to say it because it shows them that I'm simpatico and we have something in common. I don't go in there and say, "Geez, Don, what a crappy day I'm having! Can I have a chair?" There's no point to that. Don't drop your garbage in other people's yards. Make sure they always remember you as the most pleasant experience in their day. Never complain! Never complain! Never complain!

Disadvantage 4: You can't change your mind.

If you agree to an offer on a property, you cannot change your mind. You must close the deal. If you get to the offer point, it's yours. Even if you miscalculated anything, take the loss or you're toast. That needs no further explanation. There are no ifs, ands or buts about these. These are absolutes. If you violate any of these rules, you will remember me.

Disadvantage 5: You must slow down.

This relationship is very time-consuming and requires much patience. Slow down and listen. A lot of people are married. Do you want to stay married? You have to nurture your relationship. Do you have kids? Do you want your kids to listen to you? You have to take the time.

Time is going to be taken from someplace else. You have to nurture it. Any relationship in existence in this world that you do not nurture will disappear. Your relationship with your son, daughter, father, mother, aunt or the mailman, it will fall away. I see that as a disadvantage because it's time-consuming.

I want to share something with you that's very personal. I only have one son and one grandson that I adore. When my son was a young boy, he and I were very close. We often played more like kids than father and son. Due to my lack of understanding and maturity, I violated every piece of advice I have given you in these pages, and subsequently lost the closeness and depth my son and I shared. Yes, we still see each other and speak, but that closeness is gone. That is a high price to pay for ignorance. Being a workaholic, as well as valuing money and financial security above all else, can carry with it a cost higher than you may be willing to pay. It took me many years and lots of pain to learn how to understand my own behavior. It is the deep pain of that loss that helped me to change my individual conduct and behavior on how I choose to deal with anyone, everyone I meet in my life. I realized I could create love in my life and fill that void in my own heart by choosing to love others first, and I've been doing just that for years. I'm relentless about loving everyone I meet, period! I know that sounds crazy, but it makes me feel great. I suggest you do the same.

The true meaning of love and commitment is not what you may be imagining. Love is not just a feeling, a sensation. Love is a verb. It is only as deep, as real and profoundly resonating as the acts that it motivates you to dare, on behalf of those you adore. Evidence of that is given to us in our lives from all directions, nature, history, religion, individual sacrifice, and is found in all stories that have ever touched our souls.

Remember, the only love you will ever truly feel is not the one others have for you; it's the one you choose to create for others. And that, my friend, you can choose to do every minute of every day as long as you're alive.

So get ready for some hugging when we meet, and get busy loving somebody right now!

CHAPTER 33

REO Broker Secrets Revealed

What comes next is very important.

I have three separate letters from the three top REO agents (who I've been doing business with for years, and that made me a multi-millionaire) who explain, in their own words, why they chose to start working with me as a new investor, and why they ultimately stayed working with me as I became the #1 phone call they wanted to make.

These letters contain gold. Read them carefully. Pay close attention, and see if you can find parallels to what we've already covered in this book.

But first, do you know how I got these? My son came to me a few years ago and said, "I want to be an investor." Finally! I've been trying to get him to do that for 27 years. I used to talk to him in his sleep. I used to hang banners on the ceiling above his bed. He told me he never wanted to do it. Somebody else who has some influence suggested it, his girlfriend. All of a sudden, he had a paradigm shift. "Dad, I think it's cool."

I took him to all the agents. I said, "Can you guys please explain to my son why you chose to deal with me?" And this is what they said. I then went to all of them and said, "Will you put that in writing for me? Would you do me that favor?" And here they are. (I want you to understand that typically professional REO agents will not do this for anyone.)

Pay close attention. These are their fears. Get it straight. These are the things that bother them. These are their wants and needs.

Please go through these letters line by line because they are full of advice from brokers that made me financially successful, and they can do the same for you only if you read their letters carefully and take their advice. No one has ever captured this information before or since.

Letter #1: Troth Realtors GMAC Real Estate in the Antelope Valley (now Prudential Troth Realtors)

Don Anderson is one of the owners of Prudential Troth Realtors, one of the most active companies in the Antelope Valley. He's been an REO broker handling the distressed properties for over 25 years. Don was one of the first REO brokers I worked with, and he has become a really good friend. He is personally responsible for helping me make millions of dollars in profit from buying crappy little houses, most of them REOs, that nobody wanted.

Below is his letter.

To Whom It May Concern:

My business relationship with Antonio I. Alvarez (Tony) began in 1998. Tony was one of several investors purchasing homes in the Antelope Valley for the purpose of repair and resale for a profit, known in the industry as "flipping."

During the years of 1998 to 2001, I estimate that I represented Tony in the purchase of over 200 homes. During the years of 2002 through the present, I have represented Tony as a seller for 25 homes.

Tony has always closed his escrows in a timely manner, mainly due to his ongoing ability to secure financing.

Tony never made a purchase that he did not close. Many other investors would make offers tying up the property, only to cancel escrow late in the deal because of the lack of ability to secure financing, or realizing after home inspections were complete that they had made a bad purchase.

Tony benefits from his extensive knowledge of appraisals and knows going into the deal that it is financially prudent.

In the year 2000, Tony predicted a change in the market as homes began to rapidly appreciate and began keeping the homes he was purchasing as investment rental properties.

Other investors continued buying and selling during the past four years. On the 50-plus homes that Tony kept ownership of during this period, he has seen in excess of 50% appreciation. He truly watches the statistics of the marketplace like a hawk, staying on top of the trends, changes and demands. Tony is also the only large investor I have ever worked with that I have never had to appear in court on his behalf.

With the high volume of transactions, both purchases and sales, Tony experiences a potential of high exposure. He has always handled his customer home-buying relations with a great resolve. Please feel free to contact me.

Letter #2: Coldwell Banker Bozigian

Charla Abbot is a young lady who I adore. She's 50-something, married and could probably beat me up. I'm pleasant to deal with, so she loves me. I used to bring chocolate in to put in the jar on her desk. She works with another wonderful agent named Phyllis, and I was the only guy who ever went in and refilled their chocolate jar. She always remembers that. Do you know why I did it? Almonds! She never had almond chocolates in there. I wanted my stuff. Does she know that? Not to this day, and don't tell her if you call her up.

Below is her letter:

I first met Tony Alvarez in the early 1990s. At the time, I was the lead broker for Fannie Mae, Countrywide and other lenders for their REO properties located in the Antelope Valley. Handling this volume of foreclosure properties brought many investors to me. Many would cold call and want to give me their name and address. Some would write me. A few would come to my office. I would get at least five or more contacts per week from people who identified themselves as "investors."

Tony stood out. His first contact was by phone. He was sincere. He made an impression with his humor. I took the time to take his name, and I remembered him when I had a property suited for an investor. Throughout the years to follow, Tony remained top on my list. I called him first.

The reasons I stayed with him were simple. He could see past the problems. He never complained. His word was his bond. He moved quickly and without any difficulty to me. He gave me the selling commission, and always brought the property back to me for resale.

Tony understands ethics. Often, our errors and omissions insurance will not allow us to purchase our own listings. Good agents work with other good agents to buy investment properties. We do not buy our own listings.

We have a long list of investors working with us. We will always choose the investor who performs as promised, uses us as his agent, and is pleasant in his dealings.

Letter #3: Century 21 Doug Anderson

When I went in to meet J.C. Boucher, he was a referral from another REO agent, and his first response to me was, "I can't help you." I said, "Come on."

When I went in, he said, "I can't help you. I have a bunch of investors already." He already had a group of investors buying on the west side, in the nicer parts of the Antelope Valley.

But guess what? I asked the magic question. Listen carefully. This is a really tough question. "Can I ask you one question?" He said yes. "Is there anything your guys are not buying? Is there anything or any area where your favorite guys don't like to buy?" He said, "Yes. They only buy on the west side. All that other stuff on the east side is stuff we don't want to buy." He was more colorful when he said it.

I said, "Would you do me a favor? Would you call me any time you have anything on the east side?" The east side was older homes and lower income, more blue collar. I was buying anywhere. It didn't matter to me. He said, "You want to buy on the east side?" I responded, "I'll buy anywhere as long as the price makes sense." "Well, that's different. Give me your name and the best number to reach you at."

All of a sudden, I was important to him. Why? He's not making both sides of the deal on those listings that he gets on the east side. Some other outside (potential nightmare) broker is bringing in another investor who buys on the east side. I just opened up a whole part of his business that he never had.

Let me explain. Presently, he has agents buying from him. When he gets a listing, Fannie Mae doesn't differentiate. They don't call you up and say, "Which listing would you like? Do you want the nice stuff on the expensive side of town, or do you want the ghetto?" No. They say, "Here are five listings. Sell them."

I basically told him "I'll buy all the listings you have on the bad side of town where you've never sold anything directly yourself, where you represent the buyer and seller. I'll buy the ones you have to sell to people who make you sweat." And in doing so, I became his friend.

He realized that I was there to save him and put more money in his pockets, because now he was going to sell more stuff that he'd never sold. The next thing that happened was that I said to him, "By the way, do you know this other broker?" When I mentioned his name, he sat up and said, "Of course I know him." I told him, "If you want to know what I'm about, call him up. He's been working with me for a while, and I've closed several deals with him." He said, "Oh, really?" and then hit his speed dial and called the broker to confirm he knew who I was.

That did more for me than anything else. I already had a relationship with the other broker, who was a close friend of his for years (and who was instrumental in getting him approved with Fannie Mae to be an REO broker). So was it tough for me to develop a relationship with him? It wasn't. It was a piece of cake. Why? Because he's obligated to this guy, and this guy wants to keep me happy. Why? Because I keep him happy. Are you getting the web/connection thing here?

Below is his letter:

I'm a real estate broker for Century 21 Doug Anderson. I've been in the business for over 18 years. During that time, I have had the pleasure of meeting an investor by the name of Tony Alvarez who had contacted me because of my affiliation with Fannie Mae and Freddie Mac. I had several listings with both companies during the 1990s and the peak of the foreclosure market.

I spoke with Tony about some of the properties that the REO companies did not want to rehab, but wanted to sell as-is. Tony would make an offer to them through me and secure several properties. He would then rehab the properties and either sell or rent them. He did this numerous times with me and other brokers in the area. When it came time to sell, he went back to the original broker.

During that time, Tony acquired a lot of real estate and made a lot of connections in the real estate business. He then watched *the market. When it got hot again, he started to sell all the rental properties and made a very strong profit. He has purchased some of these homes for $10,000 to $20,000.*

In the years that I have known Tony, Tony has always been on top of his business and very knowledgeable in the real estate field. He is a great investor to hook up with and always closes his transactions.

Tony has always taken some really bad properties and turned them into nice homes and then resold them.

His professionalism makes people want to work with him. As his business grew, he didn't sit back and give the work or inspection of the properties over to someone else. He does it. He hires and fires the workers as needed. He is involved until the end. Tony is very active in his business. He's there to make sure the job gets done right and in a timely manner.

Who You Need to Be

These letters are more valuable than anything I've written in this book. They tell you from the horse's mouth. These are the guys that some investors are afraid to talk to.

Here are some facts to remember. Since we know agents already have many investors to work with, we must answer the all-important question: Why would they work with us? Why would they choose to work with you? You must know and understand the importance of the answer to the question, not just the question.

Don't view these people as an adversary. They're going to make you rich. If I could kiss Don on the mouth, I would. He has a mustache. I don't know if I would.

Agents will have problem properties which are tough to move. Those are the ones that will get your foot in the door. That should be clear to you. This is common sense.

Most investors want the same thing. They want the best, easy thing. That's your competition, by the way. Those are the guys who want to make it simple and easy for themselves. They do not care to solve any broker's problems. They have not learned what I have explained to you in this book.

Many successful investors with too much money soon forget who helped make them rich. They get lazy, sloppy and egotistical. They think they did it all alone and that they are geniuses. Then they go broke.

As I mentioned, I'm guilty of all the above. I know what I'm talking to you about. I have been bankrupt not once but twice in my life. I had to practice and get it right.

That's your competition. That's who I used to strive to be. I worked really hard to get to that. What waits for you at the end of that rope is destruction. Wealth generated by greed and self-centered behavior (no matter how enriching) is only temporary at best and extremely destructive at worst. It violates natural law.

Strive to be humble, friendly, helpful, pleasing and grateful. Never forget who helped you. Remember, you are a human being, and the likable, respectful person who happens to be an investor

will surely win the top spot in the agent's heart and mind and get the first call.

You're their friend. You make them look good. You make them feel good. They feel good doing this with you. You make them feel secure. They love you.

Be a problem solver. Love your agents and anyone else along the way who helps you meet your financial goals. You owe them at least that much.

You think this is fluffy. If you make $7.2 million without doing this, it will leave your hands. It will go right out again. I don't know what you're going to do. You could hold on to it with both hands or lock yourself up in a closet, because it will have no meaning for you at all. If you take my simple suggestions and do this, you'll feel like pinching yourself every day. You will live to see your wealth multiply exponentially.

Promptly take what nobody else wants, and be grateful. Never forget anyone who helps you get to where you want to go. Reward them well, and remind them how you value them. Say it to them in writing and verbally. Tell everyone you meet. Shower them with gratitude at every opportunity. Do it in public. I really don't care how you do it, but do it.

CHAPTER 34

Conclusion

Now, here is a question I have asked you to think about at various times throughout this book. Do not ignore this step! It applies to everything in your personal or business life.

Since we know agents have plenty of investors to choose from, we have to ask why they would work with us; why would they choose to work with you? I have found the answer to that question to be quite simple:

First, win their minds with your performance. Let them know you're solid, and that you have the ability to do what you say you'll do. This is performance.

Next, win their hearts with love and sincere interest in their wellbeing. This is relationship building. After all, this person is going to make you wealthy. If you do not believe that, don't start it. If you believe this guy is going to make you wealthy, what are you waiting for? It's that simple.

If you remember nothing else from this book, remember this: Love your business associates. Care about their successes as much as your own. If you love them, they will find it easy to love you back, and they will remember you always.

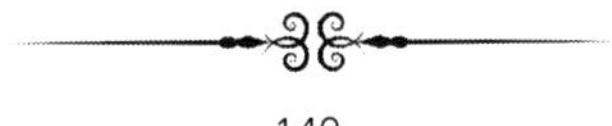

If you think this business is all about the numbers, the only deals you will ever get are the tough ones. I promise you that. If they love you, you'll not only get the deal, but you'll get them for as long as you maintain and nurture the relationship. If you nurture those relationships, you write your own ticket.

The difference in the payoff between developing long-term business friendships and just doing business for the numbers and the bucks is the difference in the payoff between flipping a property or buying it, holding it, and liquidating at the end of the appreciation at the top of the market when things start to level off.

Flipping is a short profit. It's fast. You never see the guy again. But I do. I end up with these people coming to my house afterward. We do one deal together, and they think they're family now. That's how it is for me and I would not have it any different. I love people, I love helping you and watching you grow and make my life wonderful and I love my life. I am truly blessed

I didn't make $7.2 million because I'm brilliant. I didn't make it because I'm great at public speaking. I did it because I believe in every word I'm telling you, and it has paid my way in life to do whatever it is that I want to do right now.

You really need to recognize the people that do things for you and change your life. I hope that someday you say that even the most remote thing I've written in this book has made a positive change for you in your life, like Bruce Norris's words and advice have done for me. Touching your life in a constructive and positive way is the greatest accomplishment I could ever achieve.

A Love Story

Now I'd like to share a very personal story that hopefully will help you understand what I mean by creating a bond with a perfect stranger almost immediately, by using random acts of kindness whose effects could be life-changing and last a lifetime.

Years ago, there was a very popular television show that has recently made a comeback. The show was called "Kojack," and it starred Telly Savalas. It was about a New York police detective. My son and I would watch the original show religiously. The new one, I must admit, I don't really care for because it's missing the one ingredient which I believe made the first show a success, and that was the actor, Telly Savalas. He was brutal. But he was always able to convey to everyone he dealt with that although he was tough, he truly cared for them. Kojack loved everyone, even the crooks as he locked them up. And that affection he had for people came through both onscreen and off.

Some years after the show started, my 9-year-old son and I were driving around the San Fernando Valley. I was working as an appraiser then, and I always carried a camera in the car. All of a sudden my son yells out "Kojack! Dad, it's Kojack!" And sure enough, I looked and there was Telly Savalas walking into an insurance company with another man who I later learned was his bodyguard.

I stopped the car, and as if on cue, my son grabbed the camera off the seat, jumped out of the car and ran directly at Telly Savalas yelling "Kojack! Kojack!" Telly Savalas saw my son running at him and his bodyguard moved to get between them, but Telly Savalas quickly pushed his bodyguard out of the way, reaching down with a huge smile on his face and picked my son up in his arms, hugging him, twirling around in a circle like some scene in a love story. My son was in heaven.

After some laughing and playing around, Telly Savalas handed the camera to his bodyguard and the bodyguard took a picture of them hugging. They were joking around with each other like two family members who hadn't seen each other for years. Soon after, my son came back to the car and was beaming. "Dad! Uncle Kojack said hi and how come you didn't get out for a picture? He said we can come by anytime. Did you know Uncle Kojack owns this building and he said we can come by anytime, Dad?" As we drove away, Mr. Savalas blew a kiss at my son and yelled out the signature line from his show "Hey! Who loves ya, baby?" and my son yelled back, "You do, Uncle Kojack!"

Telly Savalas did not really know my son and my son only knew the character from the television show, but somehow the character Telly Savalas played on TV connected with a huge audience across the country, and really, there's no secret to it. It's plain old LOVE! He made us open up and feel close to him. And that is exactly what turned Telly Savalas, a perfect stranger, into Uncle Kojack in minutes before my very eyes. My son felt it and, honestly, so did I. It's no wonder my son decided to become an actor.

Telly Savalas is no longer with us, but that memory still lives with my son and me. The picture of Telly Savalas and my son is still in our family photo album. I can't explain it any better than to say it made us feel good to watch that show every week. And every time my son and I remember that day, we feel something special.

Now, here's the thing. We all have that capacity to affect others whether in our personal or business lives. It's all about what actions you decide to take. It's all up to you!

Love your business associates. Remember to care about their successes as much as your own.

Tony Alvarez Jr. & Telly Savalas

Antonio —
Good Luck
Telly Savalas

Do what you must to have your business associates remember you with respect and affection, and you will, without fail, achieve much more than your financial goals.

And hey, who loves ya, baby?

Thank you for allowing me to share this time with you.

SECTION II

THE PATH OF LEAST RESISTANCE

HOW I MADE OVER $7.2 MILLION IN 7 YEARS WHILE MAKING FRIENDS

THE PATH OF LEAST RESISTANCE

INTRODUCTION

The title of this talk may seem a bit simple. Because it doesn't explain all the steps involved in getting from bankruptcy, which is exactly where I was in 1995, to the $7.2 million I've made since. Today I am going to go over everything I did. To begin with, everything I do I try to do in the simplest way. Why? Because I am basically lazy, somewhat incompetent, and I have the attention span of a flea. I like to do things quickly and easily. And the steps have to be very simple. If not, I get confused and frustrated. As you know, there are many ways to find real estate deals. As much as I can, I work with real estate brokers and agents that control foreclosures, FNMA or lender-owned properties. This I have found to be the easiest way, and with "total leverage" — that is, other people's money and other people's time. Even so, during this time my schedule was pretty packed and my cell phone never stopped. This, I believe, is the price you must be willing to pay to realize these kinds of numbers in such a short time.

LOAD YOUR G.P.S.®

1. Goal
2. Plan
3. Systems

EXAMPLE

The Goal: The Ultimate Destination
(net worth, number of properties, etc.)

My original goal was simple: To acquire $1,000,000 in net worth in 5 years with $10,000 monthly net cash flow. Buy 10 houses and pay them off - own them free and clear.

The Plan: Methods or Strategies
(how you will get there)

A. Buy, Fix and Sell

Buy houses at 50% of "After-Fix-Up Value" (AFV).
Keep buying and repair costs at 10% to 20% of AFV.
Keep carrying and selling costs at 10% to 20% of AFV.
Net profit = 10% to 30% of AFV

Example:

After-Fix-Up Value	=	$100,000
Purchase Price	=	$50,000
Buying & Repair Costs	=	$10,000 to $20,000
Carrying & Selling Costs	=	$10,000 to $20,000
Profit	=	$10,000 to $30,000

B. Buy, Fix and Hold (repair and hold as rentals to top of market)

The benefits of holding rentals:

- Less repairs; no selling costs; refinance for tax-free profits
- Stabilize/increase income cash flow

Note: May want to set up separate companies to buy and hold, and one to buy and sell.

Methods and Strategies

1. Hire a buyer's broker.

2. Get set-up to automatically receive new listings within your parameters by email. (Auto-prospecting)

3. Use hard-money lenders/other investors for acquisition capital.

4. Hire workers as employees for repairs to keep costs low. Must have enough rehab properties to keep them busy and justify overhead costs; if not, outsource or have contractors outsource.

5. Have one office assistant to handle calls and research properties.

6. Outsource bookkeeping and tax preparation. Prepare a weekly P&L and balance sheet.

7. If volume is high enough, hire an assistant to handle follow-up calls with brokers. Assistant must have the right personality.

8. Always re-list properties for sale with the agent who originally gave you the deal.

9. Buy an average of 4 to 10 purchases per month.

10. Meet new agents by doing presentations at their office meetings providing helpful tips on dealing with investors.

11. Meet all real estate agents in my local Multiple Listing Service (MLS) within 12 months.

12. Write and submit 10 offers a day, if inventory allows.

The Systems - Techniques

(daily actions, measured for results)

1. Read and review local/national news articles online 6:00 to 7:00 a.m. daily.

2. Review MLS for cancelled, pending, back on the market and short sales three times a day for new listings. 8:00 a.m., 12:00 noon, 5:00 p.m.

3. Check new listings between 8:00 to 9:00 a.m. daily.

4. Inspect new properties between 10:00 to 1:00 p.m. daily.

5. Contact agents/brokers between 1:30 and 3:30 p.m. daily.

6. Meet with new agent three times a week in person (M-W-F)

7. Write and submit offers between 4:00 and 5:00 p.m. or during the close of the day, as time allows.

8. Write activity report and results at the end of every day.

9. Go home no later than 6:00 p.m. and write to-do list for next day.

A) FINDING THE AGENTS

There are a few ways to find these agents.

1. If you have access to MLS do a search with catch words FNMA, Freddie Mac, bank owned, lender owned, REO, etc. These will list agent contact information.

2. If you do not have access to MLS, you must go to the internet and pull individual searches for each web page (FNMA, etc.) There you will find properties listed by area and the broker's information for that property.

    - www.homesteps.com
    - www.homepath.com
    - www.reobroker.com
    - www.nrba.com
    - www.car.org
    - www.realtor.org

3. New agents: Flyers, fax, or drop off to real estate office Attract newer agents with random deals, new contacts. Use title reps to deliver flyers if possible. They know the best agents.

4. A very simple method is to drive around your target market neighborhoods and call on all the available listings.

B) GETTING THE FIRST DEAL

1. Once you find a specific listing call agent directly on that specific listing. Ask the usual questions about the property. Do NOT introduce yourself as an investor looking to buy multiple homes at this time. Just focus on asking questions about that specific listing, explain if you have 1031 funds, etc.

2. Try to get a feel for the agent's personality type (friendly, helpful, dry, hostile, control freak, knowledgeable). Establish rapport by asking questions about the real estate market, their opinion etc.

3. This is your best opportunity to say, "I know you're probably very busy. How about we meet at your office later today or tomorrow?" etc.

4. If no appointment happens, then drop in within the next two days without an appointment.

5. For me, meeting face to face is crucial to my long-term success.

C) FIRST MEETING

1. Try to meet in agent's personal office. Why? This is where you get to really know what is important to them.

2. Notice what's on their desk and walls, all their trophies, family pictures, plaques and awards.

3. This gives you a deep insight into what your agent values.

4. Make conversation on what you see. Ask questions. Now is the time to make a connection.

5. Bring your resume and tools of trade. Don't leave home with out them.

    - Bank statements (if full with cash)
    - Letter of credit from lender (Norris Group)
    - 1031 exchange account balance, if any
    - Inventory of existing property you own (builds credibility)

6. Verbal resume of who you know, deals you've closed in area, and other agents you've worked with they may know. Anything that gives you credibility and makes you look good.

7. Your plans. Explain that you're looking to develop long-term relationships.

WHEN THE CALL COMES TO YOU ON THE FIRST DEAL, *FLY!*

Speed **is everything. They will be watching your every move!**

1. Respond immediately and with confidence.
2. Get back to them the same day.
3. Do not expect a great deal on the first call. After all, it will be the one none of the usual investors wanted or just were not able to get to.
4. Do not complain! The deal is what it is. Take it or leave it.
5. Be thankful and gracious whatever the outcome.
6. There will be little negotiating. Agent usually will do it all, and many times will guide you with the magic number.
7. Always perform as promised or better.
8. After you get the deal, follow up with gratitude. Go outside the deal. Do something you're not obligated to do.
9. If you can't make the deal work, explain why. Show the agent it is not workable. "But if you can help me make these numbers work, I'll buy the deal." (You'll get the second chance.)

Since we know agents already have many investors to work with, we must answer the all-important question: *Why would they work with you?*

THE SUBTLE CHANGES THAT CAN MAKE A MONUMENTAL DIFFERENCE!

1) LOVE YOUR AGENTS

"I don't necessarily have to like my players and associates, but as the leader I must love them. Love is loyalty. Love is teamwork. Love respects the dignity of the individual. This is the strength of any organization."

– Vince Lombardi

Did you ever fall in love? Seldom is it love at first sight usually one person is leading the other to falling in love.

Going Deeper by Leading the Relationship, Winning Their Hearts and Minds, Getting the Best Deals, and Getting in First Position

To get the best deals and get called first you must do two things consistently well!

A. First, you must make your agents love the way you work. How? Understand your agent's fears and eliminate them:

1. You won't close.
2. You don't know what you're doing.
3. Litigation.
4. You're inexperienced.
5. You have no money.
6. They will lose the account with the lender.
7. You'll make them look bad.

B. Understand your agent's needs and wants: Know what your agent expects from you, and give it to them! *Performance is everything. It requires speed and accuracy. ACT FAST!*

1. Trust, knowledge, experience, ability to perform, loyalty.
2. Knowledgeable buyer.
3. Buy with money and good credit.
4. Do what you say you'll do.
5. Close fast.
6. No problems/smooth transaction.
7. Agreeable buyer. Pleasant to deal with.
8. Know what you want to buy.
9. Move quickly.
10. Have cash/financing for acquisitions in place.
11. Understand repair cost accurately.

Important Notes:

- Train agent to understand what you want to buy. This will increase purchases and reduce rejections.
- List properties for sale with original agent, even if they are retired or dead!
- Remember, the agent can get full 6% commission. That's a strong motivation to control both ends of deal.
- At first, a larger deposit may give you an edge. Once you develop a solid relationship, this will not be an issue.

2) MAKE YOUR AGENTS LOVE YOU FOR WHO YOU ARE!

"When the conduct of men is designed to be influenced, persuasion, kind, unassuming persuasion, should ever be adopted. It is an old and true maxim that 'a drop of honey catches more flies than a gallon of gall.' So with men. If you would win a man to your cause, first convince him that you are a sincere friend. Therein lies the drop of honey that catches his heart — which, say what he will, is the great high road to his reason and which, once gained, you will find but little trouble in convincing him, of the justice of your cause if indeed that cause be a just one. On the contrary, assume to dictate to his judgment or to command his action, and he will retreat within himself, close all avenues to his heart and head. Such is man, and so must he be understood by those who would lead him."

— Abraham Lincoln, 1842

A. Developing solid, long-term business relationships (friendships) requires time and patience. *Slow Down!*

1. Remember to be grateful.

2. Recognize their importance to your success, and show them.

3. Be generous to them.

4. Stay in touch. Remember to keep yourself in their minds.

5. Contact and communication is paramount!

B. Take your business relationship to a deeper level.

1. Understand what is important to them personally.

    - Know their personal likes (cruise, foods, snowmobiles, RVs)
    - Know their families (children, schools, fundraisers, etc.)
    - Know what they value (charities, clubs, sports teams)
    - Chocolate!
    - Familiarity removes doubt and creates confidence.

C. Make them remember you with a smile.

1. I use humor and make them remember me as the most pleasant moment in their otherwise stress-filled day.

2. I become their break from work.

3. I make them laugh. They always smile when they see me.

4. I poke fun at myself and our business.

5. I ask about them and their families <u>first.</u>

6. I become the person they complain to about some rude investor.

7. I become their friend.

8. I say thank you whenever possible, and do it in creative ways. Do it so everyone sees!

9. Find what is unique in you, and use it.

10. Write letters of appreciation to their superiors. No other investor will.

11. Our words and actions wield tremendous ***power*** and set a tone for who we are!

D. Advantages of working with agents.

1. Deal machine – constant incoming deals.

2. No negotiating. Brokers know the bottom line (This will do the deal).

3. No searching for sellers. Agent does it.

4. **One good run in this kind of market can make your life.**

5. You can train agent to know what you want and you'll save time.

6. I had agents signing for me on super deals if I was out of town.

7. These agents don't mind you approaching other listing agents. They understand.

E. Disadvantages

1. You must spend time to train your agents to deliver what you want.

2. If you make one mistake and lose the agent, you lose a large part of your business and your reputation. ***They all talk!***

3. You can't afford any mistakes. You can't have an off day.

4. If you agree to offer on a property, you cannot change your mind. You must close, even if you miscalculated anything! ***You take the loss, or you're toast!***

5. This relationship is very time-consuming and requires much patience. ***Slow down and listen!***

(See Letters of Recommendation in Appendix C)

FACTS TO REMEMBER

A. THEM:

- Since we know agents already have many investors to work with, we must answer the all-important question: ***Why would they work with you?*** **You must know and understand the importance of the answer to this question!**
- Many investors do not like or respect these agents. They view dealing with them as a necessity only.
- Agents will have problem properties which are tough to move.

- Most investors want the same thing: ***The best, easiest deal.***
- Many successful investors with too much money soon forget who helped make them rich. They get lazy, sloppy and egotistical. They think they did it all alone. They are geniuses.

B. YOU:

- Strive to be humble, friendly, helpful, pleasing and grateful, and never forget who helped you.
- The likable, respectful person who happens to be an investor will surely win the top spot in the agent's heart and mind and get the first call.
- You're their friend. You make them look good and feel good when they think of dealing with you.
- Love your agents ,and anyone else who helps you along the way to meet your financial goals. You owe them at least that much.
- Be a problem solver. Find solutions. Put your efforts into resolving tough situations for agents. The tougher the problem, the bigger the payoff!
- Take what nobody else wants and be grateful. You will win first place in your agent's heart and mind.
- Never forget anyone who helps you get where you want to go. Reward them well, and remind them how you value them. Say it to them in writing and verbally. Tell everyone you meet. Shower them with gratitude at every opportunity.

CLOSING

As investors, we need something to give us an edge Bruce Norris calls this a tie breaker. Since we know agents have plenty of investors to choose from, we have to ask, "Why would they call you?" I have found the answer to that question to be as simple as this: If you were an agent and your family member or friend, someone who you love and care for, was an investor, who would you think of first when deciding to give away a big bag of money? Simple, isn't it?

First win their minds with your performance. Let them know you're solid, that you have the ability to do what you say you'll do. This is performance.

Next, win their hearts with love and sincere interest in their wellbeing. After all, this person is going to help you become wealthy. This is relationship building.

If you remember nothing else today, remember this: Love your business associates. Care about their success as much as yours. If you love them, they will find it easy to love you back, and they will remember you always!

If you think this business is all about the numbers, the only deals you'll get will be the tough ones.

If they like you, they'll trust you. If they trust you, you'll get the edge.

But if they love you, you'll not only get the deals, but you'll get them all for as long as you maintain the relationship.

The difference in the payoff from investing in long-term business relationships is the same as the difference in the payoff from flipping properties or buying and holding them and riding the appreciation wave to the top. I challenge you today to make it a point to meet all of the other investors in this room. Your next partner or successful business friendship may well be in this room. Don't miss it!

Years ago, there was a very popular TV show that has recently made a comeback. This show was called "Kojack," and it stared Telly Savalas. It was about a New York police detective. My son and I would watch the original show religiously. The new one, I must admit, I don't really care for because it's missing the one ingredient which I believe the first show had that made it a success: Telly Savalas. He was brutal. But he was always able to convey to everyone he dealt with that he was tough, but he truly cared for them. He loved everyone, even the crooks as he locked them up, and that affection he had for people came through.

Some years after the show started, my 9-year-old son and I were driving around the San Fernando Valley. I was working as an appraiser then, and I always carried a camera in the car.

All of a sudden, my son yelled out "Kojack! Dad, it's Kojack," and sure enough, I looked and there was Telly Savalas walking into an auto repair shop with who I later learned was his bodyguard.

I stopped, and as if on cue my son grabbed the camera off the seat and ran out of the car directly at Telly yelling, **"Kojack! Kojack!"** Telly Savalas saw my son running at him. His bodyguard moved to get between them, but Telly Savalas quickly moved his bodyguard out of the way. He reached down and, with a huge smile on his face, picked up my son and hugged him. My son was in heaven. After some laughing and joking around, Telly Savalas handed the camera to his bodyguard and the bodyguard took a picture of them hugging. They were joking around with each other like two family members who hadn't seen each other for years. Soon after, my son came back to the car and was beaming. "Dad, Kojack said hi and how come you didn't get out for a picture? He said we can come by anytime. Did you know Uncle Kojack owns this car repair shop? He said if we need repairs, to bring the car down, Dad!" As we drove away, Mr. Savalas blew a kiss at my son and yelled out, **"Hey, who loves ya, baby?"** and my son yelled back, **"You do, Uncle Kojack."**

Telly Savalas did not really know my son, and my son only knew the character from the TV show. But somehow that character Telly Savalas played on TV connected with a huge audience across the country, and really there's no secret to it. It's plain old LOVE! My son felt it, and honestly so did I.

Telly Savalas is no longer with us, but that memory still lives with my son and me. The picture of Telly Savalas and my son is still in our family photo album. I can't explain it any better than it made us feel good to watch that show every week. And every time my son and I remember that day, we feel something good.

Do what you must to help your business associates remember you with respect and affection. And you will, without fail, achieve much more than your financial goals.

And hey, who loves ya, baby?

Thank you for allowing me to spend this time with you today.

SECTION III

14 DISTINCTIONS THAT GAVE ME THE EDGE

14 Distinctions That Gave Me the Edge

There are probably many things that gave me an edge over my competition and helped me to become successful and ultimately wealthy beyond my own goals. However, the following are the 14 distinctions that I have identified as the most crucial to my success.

1. I Was Broke and Highly Motivated

Having just come through bankruptcy I didn't have a penny to my name. Not only that, but my credit was horrific and my confidence was destroyed. Basically, I had nothing to lose. Believe it or not, this is what I believe made me extremely motivated, determined and committed to succeed. I had to do it for many reasons, but mostly to prove to myself that I could overcome all the obstacles and win the brass ring.

2. I Took Immediate Action

I knew where I wanted to go, and I did not hesitate in taking action to get there. I know it sounds silly, but most people dream about where they want to go, but never take the first step to make those dreams come true. I suppose I could say I don't understand this, but the truth is I do. I understand exactly why they don't take that first step. You see, the reason I know this so well is because I've been there myself. Do you want to know why they don't do anything concrete to change their lives for the better? It's fear — plain, simple, unadulterated **fear.**

They're afraid of succeeding. They're afraid of failing. Honestly, they're just afraid, and many times they don't even know why. This is a strange phenomenon. For those of you that have wanted to get started investing or doing anything in your lives and have hesitated due to any kind of fear, I strongly suggest that you go to my website at www.tonyalvarez.com and buy the small course I designed named "Crushing the Fear Factor."

This course is a must-have for anyone who has ever taken a class or read a book about investing and never taken any action beyond that. Do yourself a favor and don't waste another dime on any other book or course until you deal with understanding and crushing your fears of taking action. This course will help you move on to making better decisions by exposing to you why your mind does what it does to keep you chained like a prisoner without taking any action. Remember, anything you ever get from me comes with a 30-day money-back guarantee.

3. My Background as an Appraiser

I understood how to identify value in a deal quickly and without hesitation. I was confident about my ability to identify a steal. This was a great advantage over my competition. The faster you can identify a deal and arrive at a confident decision, the sooner you will be able to take action and beat out your competition in submitting an accurate offer. This increases your percentage of accepted offers and decreases your rejections. In the performance side of the business, speed and accuracy is everything.

4. I Was Knowledgeable

I understood my target market thoroughly. I was extremely familiar with my market statistics. I understood the Multiple Listing Service thoroughly. I knew my rental market and if it was changing; were rents declining or increasing? I knew where to buy and where not to buy AND WHY, a decision that sometimes most investors overlook in their rabid search for the almighty "deal." I understood my market so well that I knew when the prices changed; when it was time to lower my offers or raise them to stay in tune with the present changes in the marketplace. To do this accurately, you must stay in touch with what's going on in your marketplace on a daily basis. Most investors do not.

5. I Had Initial Cash

Since I was broke, I found investors and partners for equity investments. Even though I was using hard-money lenders, I still needed money for the down payment and repair costs, at least in the beginning. I worked diligently by doing presentations to real estate offices and investor clubs, or I spoke about what I was doing as an investor in the area. I spoke about my successes and my plans. I was open about the fact that I expected to do quite well financially. This made people curious. These people had money, but they didn't have my level of knowledge. They wanted to participate, if I could convince them to like me. Then they would listen. They would trust me, and because they trusted me they would back me up. That's all I did, plain and simple. I only used investor capital for the equity portion of my investments until I was able to build up my own cash reserves.

6. I Had Financing

I used hard-money lenders as well as private investors to provide the financing on my purchases. I had to do this because I didn't have good credit, and most of the properties that I purchased were in severe disrepair, meaning that since the properties were not livable at the time of purchase no conventional lender would lend on property.

7. I Built Credibility

I quickly moved to create a reputation as the person who did exactly what he said he was going to do. I kept my word and my commitments. Early on, I made a simple, but conscious commitment to never lie to anyone that I did business with, especially the REO brokers and agents who were so kind as to start doing business with someone in my situation. This may seem simplistic and even naive, but I credit this decision with being one of the most important in solidifying my business relationships.

It was basically choosing to do the right thing regardless of the consequences. Over the years, this has paid off handsomely.

8. I Created Relationships

By now, I am sure you can see my business model encompasses a strong emphasis on creating long-term business relationships and relies on this factor as one of the keys, if not the key reason to my rapid and lasting success.

From the beginning, I proactively sought to create an interdependent team of area professionals to work with. This was not a difficult task. It was as simple as spending most of my time making friends. Many times when I speak at different investor clubs and cover the importance of building relationships, there is always someone in the audience who voices the concern about their own perceived inability to take this step and put themselves out there for the purpose of creating new business relationships — business friendships, if you will. Somehow, something in their own mind is telling them that this will not be a possibility for them, but nothing is further from the truth.

It's no different than what we do when we're kids and have to start attending a new school, or when we move to a new neighborhood, or start dating. It's all the same thing. And of course, we feel the same fears of rejection, but this is a small price to pay for what awaits us on the other side of that small challenge which is fearless living.

I strongly suggest you take a step every time and any time you have the opportunity to do so. By that, I mean every time you have the opportunity to meet someone new, to go somewhere you've never been, to expose yourself to situations that you've never experienced. What awaits you on the other side of that fear is a treasure reserved only for the courageous. Take the next step.

9. I Systemized Operations – K.I.S.

I kept things simple, and I mean really simple, clear and repeatable. Remember what I said before, I am not the sharpest tool in the shed. I am not the brightest bulb in the box. I sincerely mean this. I

do not consider myself to be the most intelligent person I have ever met. Quite the opposite. I am at best of average intelligence, and ADD to boot. So for me, simple, easy-to-understand and repeatable systems are a must. Without them, I'd be a disaster.

I want you to know, even in today's high-tech world I can barely type. I have a smart telephone, but I don't know how to use three quarters of the bells and whistles on it. I do use a computer, and as a matter of fact, I have two of them, a laptop that I take with me wherever I go, and a desktop that my assistant set up at my home in my spare bedroom/office as a "dictation station" where I'm presently dictating these pages into a wonderful software program called "Dragon Naturally Speaking" which keeps me from having to hunt and peck with two fingers on the keyboard like a madman. This program is absolutely fantastic. It actually takes my spoken words and types and them up very nicely on the pages right in front of my eyes. It's a damn miracle, and probably the only reason I ever got around to doing this book.

10. Timing

I guess it didn't hurt that I entered the real estate market at the bottom; another benefit of staying on top of my target market statistics. Most people don't get it when I tell them the value of staying on top of what's going on in their market from day to day. They really don't. Understanding when to get in the market and when to get out is a crucial component of walking away when it's all said and done with a huge amount of cash in your coffers. It's true that you can buy real estate at any time in the real estate cycle by creatively manipulating financing and other factors. You can create cash flow and turn a sow's ear into a silk purse, but there's a lot to be said for timing the market and entering at the bottom and riding the wave of appreciation all the way up until it crests. It's much like sitting on comfortable ski lift as it gently takes you up and up the mountainside for a comfortable joyride, all the while enjoying the beautiful views of snow-covered mountains.

11. Education

As I mentioned, I'm a high school dropout, but that was many years ago. Actually, I was a 19-year-old boy (It's hard to believe so much time has gone by! Today I'm 54.) Sometimes I wish I could sit with that young 19-year-old man and share with him a few things I've learned along the way. But I'm sure he wouldn't have time to listen.

The truth is that when I discovered real estate, I went back to school faster than you can sneeze. For the first time in my life, I realized I had found a way out, my ticket to freedom, and I could make it happen for myself. I focused 100% of my attention on learning everything I could about the real estate business. I took every single real estate class that I could find. I registered at junior college. I took real estate law, real estate principles, real estate appraisal, real estate everything! I bought every course I could find on investing. I watched every late-night infomercial and never hesitated to buy whatever they were selling. I threw myself into the study of real estate as if my life depended on it.

And when I wasn't studying real estate, I focused my attention on studying human nature. I found the study of the mind (the way we think and how we react emotionally) to be one of the most interesting and beneficial decisions I've ever made. It helped me to understand that only to the level that I understand myself and my own behavior, only to that level, can I hope to understand others that I meet in my life. That was a wonderful lesson and a tremendous motivator to continue my own internal studies. These studies have served me in my personal life as well as my business life.

12 – I Learned to Focus

The fact that I have ADD actually helped me focus my attention. You see, people that have ADD typically experience one of two modes. We are either hyper-focused or completely scattered. I was able to identify the specific items of my business that I needed to focus my attention on to help me function at a high level of efficiency. By this, I mean that I identified the areas in my business, which were the most important, and then I eliminated everything else. I went through a cathartic process of removing anything from my days that stole my time away.

Many times friends and business associates comment on how difficult is it to reach me or get me to respond; this is why. Knowing my limitations, I understand I MUST not break my focus for any reason or my day is gone! I seriously risk losing a whole day of productivity if I just take that call on my cell phone from a friend who's calling just to say, how ya doing?

I know it sounds crazy, but it's real. At the same time, when focused, I can hyper focus my attention so clearly that my brain has the ability to lock and load very much like a fighter pilot would on a target within his sights and actually flawlessly write or dictate an entire book or course within 24 to 48 hours. ADD has actually been a blessing in these past recent years. So you see, God knows exactly what he's doing.

I have a very good friend who is a very successful investor, writer, teacher and speaker in Southern California named Mike Cantu, and he accurately calls these time wasters "time vampires." By identifying and synthesizing specific areas and actions to focus my attention on, I was able to eliminate anything else that was basically a huge waste of time and a distraction from my core business. My day was divided between staying on top of my target market, making my offers and inspecting properties on a daily basis, and contacting people in my business life with whom I had developed or wanted to develop business relationships/friendships and who were interested in doing the same with me. Everything else got kicked to the curb.

13 – I Managed My Own Properties

The most impactful and profitable decision I've ever made in my real estate investment career was when I decided to switch from just buying and selling single family residences to buying and holding them as rental properties. This one change not only assured me of a consistent increase in my monthly income, but over time it exploded my net worth beyond my wildest dreams. Buying and selling real estate can make you a tremendous income and provide a good lifestyle, but only buying and holding rental properties can make you filthy rich. The key is to have a solid in-house management system.

I do not believe in using management companies to manage my real estate. I did try it, and quickly found out it was not for me. It was lacking in too many things that I consider important and vital to long-term success as a long-term real estate investor. At first, property management was difficult, and we made many mistakes.

As a matter of fact, I think I made just about every mistake possible. And when I was finished with those, I invented some new ones. One of the most important distinctions I made was that I was not necessarily in the property management business as much as I was in the people business. To be honest, it took me quite a few years of learning from my mistakes and studying every real estate management course I could get my hands on to get it right, but we got it right.

Actually, we got so good at managing our properties that at our busiest time (and with only one assistant) I was able to manage up to 100 single-family homes while still keeping my home buying business at a minimum of one house a week. Managing our properties simply became as easy as eating a bowl of ice cream. Now keep in mind that we rent to all different kinds of tenants from all different economic circles. We specialize in renting to government-subsidized Section 8 tenants such as seniors and single mothers, as well as blue-collar workers and aerospace engineers and everything in between. Our rentals are well diversified in all kinds of neighborhoods, with tenants from all different levels of the economic scale. This is what has made our management system, as well as our own monthly rental income, so solid.

We have, what I like to call a front-loaded system. Our marketing and screening process is so tight, so good, that we eliminate potential problems long before they can ever develop into anything time-consuming or serious. This takes knowledge and actual hands-on experience working with literally thousands of potential rental applicants over the past 29 years. The bottom line is we never rent to anyone who we wouldn't have over to our home for lunch or anyone we would never want to have as a next-door neighbor.

Obviously, there's a lot more to property management than what I've explained, but the most important distinction I want you to make is this: If you want to stabilize and consistently grow your monthly income (while your net worth grows almost effortlessly), buying and holding rental properties is the only way to go, and it's the biggest reason why I ended up making $7.2 million in 10 years. If you're curious or have any questions, or if you would just like to have a free peek at a portion of our actual property management course materials or hear a portion of the audio CD version of our course titled "Manage Your Way to Millions," please go to www.TonyAlvarez.com and click "Take a Free Peek."

14. Mentors and Consultants

Whether you are aware of it or not, you have mentors. We all have mentors. But here is an important question to ask yourself: Did you choose yours, or did you just end up following someone out of some kind of accident or strange luck? You see what I mean? It's true! When you think back to high school or even grammar school, we all admired or emulated someone we wanted to be like.

The problem is that most of us never learned to actively choose someone who we calmly decided was worth following or emulating; for good reason. Sometimes it just feels embarrassing to admit that at 20, 30, 40 or even 54 years of age like me, you still need to listen or watch the behavior of another person to correct your own. We all like to think of ourselves as independently invincible, but we are not.

True mentors are vitally important to saving you time and money, and can typically catapult your results in any area quickly and to much higher rates of return than doing it alone. **Notice I said TRUE mentors. There is a difference.**

An imposter will just take your money, waste your time and will know little more than you, which will ultimately confuse you and actually delay your progress. Therefore, the process of choosing a mentor should be taken with care.

I have always been someone who likes to see himself as riding alone, doing everything independently of others so to speak, but nothing is further from the truth. All of us rely on others for help and guidance – ALL OF US!

Over the years, I have been fortunate to meet wonderful people in and out of the real estate business. Most of my business acquaintances have over time become business friends. And those relationships have become invaluable and gone on to help me tremendously to accomplish my financial goals.

For example, take Bruce Norris. I met Bruce years ago when he was working as a real estate investor and beginning to teach on how and when to buy. In other words, how to better position yourself to take advantage of changes that occur in the real estate cycles. Well, it was not long before we became very good friends. As time passed, Bruce got more and more involved in analyzing data, and he created a company that has gone on to become one of the best (if not the best) real estate resources in Southern California for investors and real estate professionals alike called The Norris Group.

The Norris Group is a family-run business manned by some of the best qualified, most knowledgeable, caring people you could ever find under one roof. This wonderful group of professionals provides top-quality, real-life-based education on investing and forecasting economic changes impacting the overall real estate market and investors. They provide equity loans and eight-year longer term financing for investment properties specifically for you and me when nobody else will. They have gone on to develop real estate projects, and Bruce himself does a weekly radio program where he has interviewed everyone from top real estate and business professionals like Peter Schiff to local successful investors, top REO brokers, economists, and even the FBI, and all done in a constant effort to give real estate investors an edge.

This is a company that basically specializes in how to make millionaires in real estate (I being one of them), and the top guy is my good friend and mentor, Bruce Norris. How can you beat that? To those of you reading this that have heard me speak or teach, it's no great secret that there was a point in my investment career when my net worth had already exceeded $3 million and I was considering retiring from real estate altogether. But after a brief conversation with Bruce Norris where I shared my plans, he basically said 10 words to me that changed my direction and went on to make me an additional $3 million in the following 36 months. Can you imagine that? One conversation, 10 words, $3 million... that's $300,000 a word! Talk about the value of having a **TRUE** mentor!

Everyone at The Norris Group is top notch. Bruce's two sons, Aaron Norris (who is a marketing genius, a good-hearted, wonderful person, and is always just one phone call away) and Greg Norris (who heads the acquisitions department, and who with one 10-minute conversation at one of their events this year thoroughly explained to me the insider buying secrets and benefits of buying foreclosures at the courthouse steps, where you can find him just about every morning.) Craig Hill, who heads up their lending team, is one of the brightest minds in lending, as well as a true example of a single-minded, purposeful individual. This guy knows more about loans than I do about food — and that's a lot! And let's not forget all the other wonderful people on their staff; Diana, Rhonda, Vickie, Alisha and Robyn consistently bend over backwards to help us all do better in the real estate game. And by the way, if you're looking to invest money in trust deeds, who better to give your money to than professionals that are in the game every day? These are GREAT folks! Check them out at www.thenorrisgroup.com. That decision just might end up making you a few extra bucks as well. Tell them Uncle Tony sent ya!

Bruce Norris and Tony Alvarez

You should know by now, I don't have just one mentor. I have many, and most have had absolutely nothing to do with the real estate business.

The following is a list of special people that I have considered mentors and have influenced my life.

My mother, Rina Alvarez: "If you love people, then you will know that you can do anything you want to do, become anyone you want to become, meet and make close friends with anyone in this life, no matter how important or powerful. No matter where you come from or your situation, there are no limitations in this life. NONE!" Mom is the best example of love, kindness, and determination I have ever known.

My father, Antonio Alvarez, Sr.: "Work hard, work hard, and then keep working hard!" I love you, Dad!

My older brother, Al Alvarez: He's a now-retired undercover narcotics officer from LAPD, after 25 years. Al taught me courage.

To my extended family, **Joseph & his lovely wife Joan (Mo)** Morrison, who at an early age taught me by example the value of appreciation and acceptance of others regardless of popular opinion. Thank you for your kindness.

Det. Joseph St. Germaine: He was the first police officer I ever met, and he taught me integrity.

Victor Ayala: My first employer and business partner in L.A., who taught me determination.

Al Rudolph: He was the first supervisor at my first job in L.A., who taught me how to negotiate.

Bruce Norris: One of my closest friends and a successful investor, teacher, speaker, lender, GENIUS who provided my first speaking opportunity and wrote the foreword for this book.

Mike Cantu: He is one of, if not the best wholesale house buyer in the country, as well as a teacher, speaker, good friend and trusted confidant.

Bill Tan: Owner of one of the largest real estate clubs in Southern California, one of my best buddies, and a soft-spoken, good-hearted creative genius who specializes in solving complicated real estate transactions and might even lend you a little money every once in a while.

Jack Fullerton (Coach): A good friend and solid American patriot, he is the owner of one of the oldest and most respected true real estate clubs in Southern California who is a sincere old-school investor and man of integrity that has taught us all a few things about proper judgment in our business and personal affairs (by example). And who once asked me (what I thought was a silly question at the time) about my "leaky bucket" and made me re-think the whole accounting process in my business, and went on to save me hundreds of thousands of dollars. Thank you, Jack!

All of these people have been, to one extent or another, influential in my life, and have helped me to become not only a better investor, but a better man. I sincerely love them all.

Seek true mentors and consultants. Make it a point to make them your close friends. You won't soon regret it.

SECTION IV

Hitting the Streets to Make Millions

"A truly good book teaches me better than to read it. I must soon lay it down, and commence living on its hint. What I began by reading, I must finish by acting."

- Henry David Thoreau

Take the Next Step

If you are interested in taking the next step and finding out if this wonderful business is for you, just go to our website at **www.tonyalvarez.com** and click the **FREE STARTER KIT** tab.

This will give you everything you need to get started today.

3 Steps to Getting Started

1. Download Your Free Starter Kit
2. Listen to the Audio Files and Fill Out Forms
3. Hit the Streets and Go See Houses

Free Starter Kit Includes:

"Making Millions with REOs" – Special Report (audio & ebook)

1. Opportunity of a Lifetime
2. About the Business
3. Set Your Mind Set
4. Self-Evaluation Form

   - Strengths and Weaknesses – what you have to work with
     Internal: personal, education, experience, etc.
   - Identifying and Filling in the Gaps
     External: cash, financing, contractors, etc.

5. G.P.S.® Form

This starter-kit has been especially designed for the new investor. However, if you are a seasoned investor you can also use it to give yourself a kick in the pants and to "get real" with your investing business.

Look. I know how to do this business. I understand the best and most efficient methods of doing this business successfully (most of which I've shared with you in this book), but if you don't take action, what's the point? We came this far together. Let's do this thing. Let's finish it!

The above steps are designed to help you evaluate, designate and motivate yourself to **TAKE THE NEXT STEP**.

So what are you waiting for?

Let's get started!

We have lots to do!

SECTION V

THE THIRD ELEMENT

"The feel is real, but the why is a lie."

- Guy Finley

FEAR

How do you deal with your fears?

The biggest problem facing most folks that want to get started in the real estate investing game is not lack of money, time, knowledge, education, financing, contacts or connections or even the support of their spouse and love ones. It's actually plain old unadulterated fear; it's fear of the unknown, and just as often, fear of the known. Confused yet? Please keep reading...

This situation is usually created by our own minds imagining some unwanted outcome or creating one of several obstacles which our mind see as "real" and then projecting that situation as a fix picture or movie which we then view repeatedly until we are frozen with fear. We accept this as "The Truth" and act accordingly by moving immediately to non-action and remaining there, sometimes indefinitely.

Typically, the only action we will allow ourselves to take is the "all too safe" sign-up for another class or seminar because this gives us the sensation of "doing something" and feeds our need to do the next thing (even if it's just repeating the same behavior.) Most seminar sales companies understand this human psychological condition and most marketing is built around exploiting and capitalizing on this condition.

First, they tell you that you have a problem – you're too fat, too poor, too wrinkled, too old, you need a pizza, a new dress, jewelry, car, or a trip to Fiji via some cruise line. Then they agitate the problem until you want to burst from the psychological pain by reminding you of how miserable you are and how much your life just plain sucks because you don't own their new thingamajig. Then they sell you the solution that will solve your problem forever, of course for the reduced price of whatever and the next thing you know you're running to the phone and giving some woman from Pakistan the last 4 digits of your credit card for the new and improved version of Carlton Sheets No Money Down, or whatever.

Tony Alvarez and Guy Finley

I actually bought his course twice; once with the original blue cover and then when he changed it to black a couple of years later, thinking it was new stuff. That's how stupid I can be.

Oh, you thought I was immune to this condition I just described? No way! Sometimes I think I invented it and that's why I understand it so well. Actually, the truth is a few years ago I was introduced to a book called "The Secret of Letting Go" written by Guy Finley. That wonderful book introduced me to my own mind and the tricks that it had been playing on me for years, and with my cooperation I might add.

That book changed the way I see my life and I began an internal journey for me that has yet to end. It opened the doors to understanding my own mind and to the fact that my thoughts (although undeniably occurring in my mind) are not exactly in my best interest, nor am I necessarily in control of my responses to them.

If you have ever taken a class or seminar, or even just read a book on something your heart moved you to experience and then found yourself NOT following through and taking action to DO something about it. If all you did was well up with a billion fears and reasons why it won't work or why you can't this or that, I strongly suggest you invest a bit of your time investigating your own thoughts. Ask why your own mind would keep you a prisoner of your fears instead of helping you see through them. Learn to take "right" action and end the cycle of "wrong" response.

Please go to our website at www.TonyAlvarez.com and click on Courses & Classes. I have created a small inexpensive course called "Crushing The Fear Factor." Below are some of the highlights in the book.

- All fears are not created equal -- Learn the difference between physical fear and psychological fear.
- Understand the elements of ACTION VS. NON-ACTION.
- Learn to identify the "missing link" in your inability to MAKE QUICK DECISIONS.
- Learn how to quickly identify the "enemy" and crush their power over your mind.
- SMASH the "what if" factor, forever! Free yourself from second-guessing every decision you make.
- Find your "motivating factor" to help propel you to financial heights beyond your imagined goals.

Please don't spend another penny on books, courses and classes or any of those $10,000 to $50,000 boot camp trainings that promise to make you a millionaire in a weekend nonsense until you read and listen to that short course. It will save you a ton of money. Also, if you're interested in learning more about Guy Finley and his writings please go to www.guyfinley.org. They have a great starter kit full of all kinds of free information. I love his work and highly recommend you check it out.

Remember, you don't have to spend a fortune to learn how to make one in real estate.

APPENDIX A:
FREE RESOURCES AND LINKS

Banks

Use these websites to search REOs and REO agents in your area. There are a variety of ways to search with each bank. For example, you can search by state, county, city, zip code, property description and even price. Once you have chosen a property you are interested in, simply click on the listing to see more of the property description, details and the agent/broker's contact information.

mortgage.chase.com/pages/shared/gateway.jsp *

www.grpcapital.com *

www.ocwen.com *

https://www9.bankofamerica.com/home-loans/overview.go *

(Bank of America)

http://www.usbank.com/cgi_w/cfm/personal/products_and_services/reoPropertiesReq.cfm

www.firstfedca.com *

www.pasreo.com/pasreo/public/propertySearch.do * (Wells Fargo)

www.owb.com/default.aspx?id=1178 * (Indy Mac)

Fannie Mae & Freddie Mac

These sites are user-friendly and offer a lot of useful information. The thing we like most is that you are able to sign up and receive emails when they update their inventory list with new REOs. You will get a list of available properties in your area. The listing details will provide the contact information for the agent.

www.fanniemae.com *

www.homepath.com *

www.freddiemac.com *

www.homesteps.com *

Asset Management Companies

These properties are also listed in the individual bank websites. We provide these websites even though Tony HATES going directly to the asset managers. It's a waste of time. You will get redirected to the listing agent.

www.agpassetmanagement.com *

www.lendersreo.com *

www.pasreo.com (Wells Fargo)

www.assetman.com *

www.reoworld.com *

www.bankassetmanagement.com *

Find an REO agent/Broker

Use these sites to help find a local REO agent/broker in your market area.

www.reobroker.com *

www.car.org

www.nrba.com

www.assignreo.com

www.realtor.org

Government Owned Property

Use these sites to find government owned property. You can search just your market area.

www.homesales.gov

www.hud.gov/homes/index.cfm *

www.resales.usda.gov

www.usda.gov

www.usa.gov

www.hcd.ca.gov

Search for REO Listings and Data

Keep track of the foreclosures in your area. Some of the sites even break down by pre-foreclosure, auction and bank owned. This can be very useful when trying to figure out your market area.

www.realtytrac.com *
www.hudforeclosed.com
http://hudhomes.foreclosure.com
www.bankhomesdirect.com
www.buybankhomes.com
www.foreclosure.com
www.hudpemco.com
www.reoexperts.net
www.foreclosuredata.com
www.foreclosurelistings.com
www.reonationwide.com
www.foreclosureradar.com *
www.theforeclosedhomes.com
www.realtystore.com
www.hudexchange.com
www.all-foreclosure.com *
www.reoworld.com
www.freeforeclosurereport.com
www.foreclosuredatabank.com
www.findforeclosureproperties.com
www.realestate.yahoo.com/Foreclosures

Property Profiles

This site is great if you do not have access to the MLS, but remember, this is not all the information you need. Active and pending listings are not usually listed.

Create a free account with Advantage Title and have access to run your own property profiles, get comparables, and access many real estate forms.

www.PropertyShark.com

Useful Website You MUST Check Out

www.wiestrealty.com *
Many useful items on this site to help with mortgage questions and payment breakdowns.

Property Comparables

Use these sites to find property comparables in your area. Keep in mind that some of these sites will only list the sold comparables.

www.zillow.com

www.ziprealty.com

www.valuemyhouse.com

www.trulia.com

www.rentometer.com

www.zilpy.com

www.rentbits.com

Area Stats

Use these sites to get all kinds of statistical information from the federal government and other data sources. You can find economic information, population trends, crime rates, education information, housing rates, cost of living, employment and more. This can be very useful in gathering information in your market area.

www.chamberofcommerce.com *

www.city-data.com *

www.fedstats.gov

www.bls.gov

www.bea.gov

www.bestplaces.net

www.terabitz.com

www.usa.gov *

Real Estate Forms

Use this site to find real estate forms.

www.firsttuesday.us/

Find Real Estate News & Headlines

www.inmannews.com

www.realestatejournal.com *

www.wsj.com *

www.ired.com

www.buyincomeproperties.com

www.realtytimes.com

www.investmentpropertiesinfo.com

Find Financial & Economic News & Headlines

www.money.com

www.finance.yahoo.com

www.forbes.com

www.economist.com

Find Lenders in Your Area

Use these sites to find lenders in your area. Get current interest rates for all loan types.

www.mortgage101.com

www.mortgage-investments.com

Hard-Money Loans

www.thenorrisgroup.com

Find an Escrow Company

www.ceaescrow.com

Find and Appraiser

www.appraisers.com

www.appraiserusa.com

www.sureson.com

Find a Home Inspection Company:

www.homeinspections-usa.com

www.nahi.org

Find Real Estate investors Club in California:

Eric Siragusa of San Diego	www.nsdrei.org *
Bill Tan of San Diego	www.sdcia.com *
Jack Fullerton of Orange County	www.commonwealthofoc.com *
Iris Veneracion of Irvine	www.investclubforwomen.com *
Nick Manfredi of the Inland Empire	www.ieinvestorsforum.com *
Shawn Watkins of Orange County	www.investorsworkshops.com *
Steve Love of Los Angeles	www.irca-losangeles.com *

Education:

Bruce Norris	www.thenorrisgroup.com *
John Schaub	www.johnschaub.com *
Mike Cantu	www.mikecantu.com *
Jay P. DeCima	www.fixerjay.com *
Bill Tan of San Diego	www.sdcia.com *
Jack Miller	www.cashflowconcepts.com
Rick Harmon aka the Probate Guy	www.ricktheprobateguy.com

Legal Websites:

Use these sites to find government resources, state and local laws.

www.statelocalgov.net

www.irs.gov

www.alllaw.com

www.findlegalforms.com

www.legalwiz.com

www.nolo.com

www.skipease.com (free people search and public records network)

www.legalhomeforms.com (over 40 of the most needed forms and contracts)

www.amerilawyer.com *

Real Estate Chat Rooms:

These websites offer free real estate information and articles.

www.creonline.com

www.dealmakerscafe.com/forum/

www.tonyalvarezblog.com

Find Your Local Newspaper:
Use these sites to find newspapers all over the United States. Keeping up with your local area's real estate news in very important.

www.newspapers.com

www.newsvoyager.com

www.onlinenewspapers.com

www.newspaperlinks.com

1031 Exchange Information:
Get information on 1031 exchanges and options.

www.1031exchangeforprofit.com

www.irs.gov (search for 1031 exchange)

Free Information & Tips on Rehabbing & Renovation:

www.thisoldhouse.com
www.work.com

www.doityourself.com

www.easy2diy.com

www.onthehouse.com

www.homedepot.com

www.homerepair.about.com

www.improvenet.com

www.lowes.com

Tracking Website

www.google.com/analytics

Free Maps & Driving Directions:

www.maps.google.com *

www.mapquest.com *

www.bing.com/maps

http://msrmaps.com

www.maps.com

www.globalexplorer.com

www.nationalatlas.gov

www.earth.google.com *

Hazard Mapping Searches:

Use these websites to find seismic zones and flood maps for the U.S.

www.earthquake.usgs.gov/ *

www.fema.gov *

Internet Marketing

Use these websites to help market your investing business online.

www.GetWebMedia.com

Soft Money Resource

www.lendingclub.com

www.virginmoneyus.com

www.prosper.com

Social Networks

www.facebook.com

www.linkedin.com

www.plaxo.com

www.twitter.com

Add Website to Search Engines

www.google.com/addurl/?continue=/addurl

siteexplorer.search.yahoo.com/submit

www.bing.com/docs/submit.aspx

Virtual Flyer Resources

www.vflyer.com

www.postlets.com

Research Resources

www.alexa.com (website ranking)

www.redfin.com

www.ziprealty.com

www.realtor.com

Software Tools

www.sourceforge.net/projects/freemind/ (Freemind planning software)

www.openoffice.org

Keyword Tool

www.wordtracker.com (keyword research)

www.goodkeywords.com

Press Release Outlets

www.1888pressrelease.com

www.prweb.com

Outsourcing Resources

www.elance.com

www.scriptlance.com

www.rentacoder.com

www.guru.com

www.getafreelancer.com

Article Outlets

www.ezinearticles.com

www.articledashboard.com

www.article99.com

www.isnare.com

www.articlebiz.com

www.goarticles.com

Video Channels

www.youtube.com

www.revver.com

www.vimeo.com

www.guba.com

The Third Element

www.guyfinley.com/Welcome/9/CD1607/389 * (Strongly Recommended)

www.anewlife.org

www.eckharttolle.com

www.kvie.org

* *Resources we use on an ongoing basis*

APPENDIX B: Sample Letter of Commitment

APPENDIX B

SAMPLE LETTER OF COMMITMENT

April 29, 2010

To Whom It May Concern:

Re: Tony Alvarez

The Norris Group has APPROVED a private party, hard-money purchase loan for the above mentioned borrower, not to exceed $500,000 subject to 20% down. Included with this letter, you'll find buyer's proof of funds, exceeding our 20% down requirement.

Because this is a private hard-money product, typical pre-requisites such as...property condition, buyer credit or income to loan ratios DO NOT APPLY for this product. We have funded many transactions for this client and can easily close this transaction within 30 days assuming a clear title report, accurate escrow instructions and complete buyer vesting are provided no later than two weeks prior to close of escrow date.

If you have any questions, please don't hesitate to call Craig Hill at 951-780-5856.

Thanks,

Craig Hill
Loan Manager
The Norris Group
6391 Magnolia Ave. Ste C.
Riverside, CA 92506
(951) 780-5856 phone
(951) 780-9827 fax

APPENDIX C:
Letters of Recommendation

April 20, 2005

Ref: Antonio I. Alvarez

To Whom It May Concern:

My business relationship with Antonio I. Alvarez(Tony) began in 1998 as Tony was one of several investors purchasing homes in the Antelope Valley for the purpose of repair and resale for a profit. Known in the industry as flipping.

During the years of 1998-2001 I estimate that I represented Tony in the purchase of over 200 homes. During the years of 2002- through the present I have represented Tony as seller for over 25 homes.

Unlike many other investors I have represented, Tony has always closed his escrows in a timely manner, mainly do to his ongoing ability to secure financing. Tony never made a purchase that he did not close. Many other investors would make offers tying up the property only to cancel escrow late in the deal because of the lack of ability to secure financing or realizing after home inspections were complete that they had made a bad purchase. Tony benefits from his extensive knowledge of appraisal and knows going into a deal that it is financially prudent.

In the year 2000 Tony predicted a change in the market as homes began to rapidly appreciate and began keeping the homes he was purchasing as investment rental properties. Other investors continued buying and reselling during the past four years. On the 50 plus homes that Tony kept ownership of during this period he has seen in excess of 50% appreciation. He truly watches the statistics of the market place like a hawk, staying on top of trends or changes in demand.

Tony is also the only large investor that I have worked with, that I have never had to appear in court on his behalf. With the high volume of transactions both purchases and sales Tony experiences the potential of high exposure. He has always handled his customer (home buyer) relations with great resolve.

Please feel free to contact the undersigned should any additional information be required or any explanation of any of the above statements.

Don L. Anderson – Co Owner
Troth V Inc.
Dba: Troth Realtors/GMAC Real Estate

1801 West Avenue K., Suite 101, Lancaster, CA 93534
Office: (661) 948-4646 Fax: (661) 945-9133 www.trothgmac.com

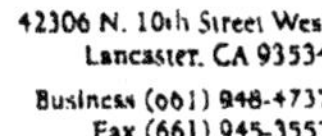

April 21, 2005

To whom it may concern,

I first met Tony Alverez in the early 1990's. At the time, I was the lead broker for Fannie Mae, Freddie Mac, Countrywide and other lenders, for their reo properties located in the Antelope Valley.

Handling this volume or foreclosed properties brought many "investors" to me. Many would cold call me and want to give me their name and address, some would write me, and a few would come to my office. I would get at least 5 or more contacts in a week from people who identified themselves as "investors".

Tony stood out. His first contact was by phone. He was sincere and made an impression with his humor. I took the time to take his name and I remembered him when I had a property suited for an investor.

Throughout the years to follow, Tony remained top on my list and I called him first for properties. The reasons I stayed with him were simple. He could see past problems, his word was his bond, he moved quickly and without any difficulty to me, he gave me the selling commission and always brought the property back to me for resale.

Tony understands that ethics and often our errors and omissions insurance, will not allow us to purchase our own listings. Good agents work with other good agents to buy investment property, we do not buy our own listings. We have a long list of investors to pass off our best buys and will always choose the investor that performs as promised, uses us as their agent and is pleasant in all dealings.

In 25 years of business, I know no better investor to teach people in the skills of investing than Tony Alverez.

Charla Abbott
Broker Associate

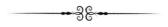

Each Office Is Independently Owned And Operated.

Doug Anderson & Assoc., Inc.
1727 W. Avenue K, Suite 102
Lancaster, California 93534
Business (661) 945-4521
Fax (661) 948-4307

April 28, 2005

To Whom It May Concern:

I am a Real Estate Broker for Century 21 Doug Anderson. I have been in this business over 18 years now. During that time I had the pleasure of meeting an investor by the name of Tony Alvarez, who had contacted me because of my affiliation with Fannie Mae and Freddie Mac. I had several listings with both companies during the late 90's in the peak of the foreclosure market.

I spoke with Tony about some of the properties that the REO companies did not want to rehab but wanted to sell as is. Tony would make an offer to them through me and secured several properties. He would then rehab the property and either sell or rent them. He did this numerous times with me and other brokers in the area. When it came time to sell he went back to the original broker. During that time Tony acquired a lot of real estate and made a lot of connections in the real estate business. He then watched the market and when it got hot again he started to sell all those rental properties and made a very strong profit. He had purchased some of these homes for as little as 10,000 to 20,000 and then sold them for 3 to 5 times that amount.

In the years that I have known Tony he has always been on top of his business and very knowledgeable in the real estate field. He is a great investor to hook up with and always closes his transactions. Being a broker for the REO companies is a major account and you didn't want just any investor coming in with offers and then not finishing the deal. That went against you with the REO companies. It was a very difficult time and very competitive market. Tony has taken some real bad properties and turned them into nice homes and then sold them.

His professionalism makes people want to work with him. As his business grew he didn't sit back and give the work or inspections of the properties over to someone else he does it. He hires and fires (if needed) the workers. He is involved until the end. Tony is very active in his business. He is there to make sure the job gets done right and in a timely matter.

Best Regards,

J.C. Boucher

N. R. VANTINE, CPA, LTD

CERTIFIED PUBLIC ACCOUNTANTS

N. R. (ROCKY) VANTINE, CPA — vantinenr@sbcglobal.net
RICK BARRETT, CPA — barrettrick@sbcglobal.net
SHERRI K. CHILDS, CPA — childssherri@sbcglobal.net
JANET HENDERSON, OFFICE ADMINISTRATOR — jshenderson@sbcglobal.net
CORLIEN ROBERTS, ASSISTANT OFFICE ADMINISTRATOR — robertscorlien@sbcglobal.net

May 19, 2005

To Whom It May Concern:

I had the privilege of meeting Antonio Alvarez in 2004 as a result of real estate acquisitions he was making in Northwest Arkansas. My expertise as a certified public accountant is in the real estate field with special emphasis in IRC Section 1031 exchanges, and during the past year I have represented Tony in several such transactions. I now serve as his tax accountant as well.

It has been fascinating watching Tony work, and it is obvious how he has achieved the financial success he enjoys. His combination of intelligence, integrity, personality and energy combine to **make** success happen. With net worth approaching ten million dollars, Tony is constantly assessing markets for opportunities created by appreciation, financing, timing, or area growth. Tony's strategies have taken him across the country researching and honing in on projects that now include commercial as well as residential real estate. He is generous in sharing his approach to business and is absolutely the best net worker I have ever met. Tony has introduced me to key people in my own hometown who have proven to be profitable contacts for my firm.

Tony knows his business; he knows himself and is quick to use professionals when dealing with issues that require their areas of expertise. I look forward to a long personal and professional relationship with Tony, and I look forward to learning from him along the way.

Sincerely,

Norman R. Vantine, CPA

302 S. 7th St., Suite A, P.O. Box 906 • Rogers, AR 72757-0906 • (479) 631-0275 • (479) 631-8973 FAX

APPENDIX D:
FLYER EXAMPLE

SELL US YOUR DOGS!

WE NEED HOUSES, CONDOS, APARTMENTS!
FIXERS & DISASTERS WITH OR WITHOUT TENANTS!

HERE'S WHAT WE DO:

1 - We are experienced Investors with ***TOO MUCH CASH*** on hand.
2 - ***We buy ALL CASH! AS IS! – NO CONTINGENCIES!***
3 – **FAST CLOSE 15 days or less** or according to Sellers needs.
4 - **We pay all costs,** if needed.
5 - We are **flexible** and **reasonable.**
6 - We have been doing business in the Antelope Valley since 1995 ***WITHOUT LITIGATION.***
7 - We have **bought *and sold millions* of dollars in Real Estate** in the Antelope Valley and have ***ALWAYS CLOSED OUR TRANSACTIONS!***
8 - We have worked with most of the **Top Brokers and Agents** in the Antelope Valley, and **we sincerely appreciate your help.**
9 - ***Letters of recommendation are available upon request.***

IF YOU HAVE TOUGH TO SELL LISTING'S, FIXERS, DISTRESSED PROPERTIES, PROBLEM PROPERTIES OR PROBLEM SITUATIONS,

DON'T MISS OUT SELL IT TO US AND MAKE YOUR FULL 6 % COMMISSION!

CALL TONY ALVAREZ (24/7) AT

(Note: Although we are licensed to sell & appraise Real Estate in California we are only interested in purchasing your listings as principles.)

WHAT OTHERS ARE SAYING ABOUT TONY ALVAREZ

Mike Cantu and Tony Alvarez

Tony, you inspired me to no end! Every time I hear you speak, I go home and revise my goals upward, way up! A morning very, very well spent. Thanks so much for sharing and holding nothing back. It's refreshing to hear the real deal from someone who's in the trenches daily. I loved all of it. Thanks again, Tony.

Mike Cantu

Hi, my name is Peter Apostolos and I'm from Los Angeles, California. I'm out in the field in the REO market and the things that Tony teaches in his seminars is beyond the spreadsheet. It's beyond the numbers. It's very easy for us that are out there investing to really get caught up in statistics and technicalities but to really ascend above that and create these relationships with agents and recognize them as people who have needs and build friendships and create those relationships that really help us transact. I've been doing kind of what Tony says for the last month or so, and it has really changed my business and really solidified my team and, more than anything, just my attitude and my confidence in what I'm doing. So, I really want to thank Tony.

Peter Apostolos

Well, what happened is we had made 250 offers, my partner and I, on properties that were REOs. And we couldn't figure it out. We thought for sure we'd have a bunch of those accepted, but they weren't getting accepted. So, anyway, after going to Tony's seminar, he said, "Maybe I need to take a look at your contracts, your offers. There's something wrong." So I faxed them over to Tony. And that's exactly what the issue was. We actually had had a callback on one of these offers that we made several weeks prior that fell out of escrow. Tony had looked at it and said, "Change this, change this, and change this." So what I changed was number one, we made sure we had a larger down than we did last time. One of the letters from a lending source didn't even have a dollar amount on it. Tony says, "That's crap! Get rid of it." So we got rid of it. We resubmitted that offer, and got that property. We revised the offer and bought the house for $161,500. We ended up putting about $60,000 into it. We're in escrow. It's gonna close any day now for $345,000. Profit on this house will be about $75,000. We did better than we expected. Thank you, Tony, for making this deal happen!

John Ulsher

I liked the down to earth approach and real examples used. I liked the practical steps in the book.

Caroline H.

I cannot believe the amount of detail that Tony Alvarez is giving us with regards to this class. He's giving us phenomenal detail. He's giving us everything that you could possibly wanna know. I have to give this class an A++ with regards to content. And he's giving it to us nice and simple so that we can understand it and absorb it, and why he's doing such a generous, generous thing for us putting us in the real estate business and giving us basically the same knowledge that he has is beyond my comprehension. All I can say is the man is phenomenal and the course is even more phenomenal. And anyone who has a chance to take his course and doesn't, should be shot!"

V. Ahda Sands

After going through the BEST real estate seminar EVER with you on Saturday, I'm very excited. The properties I've had success with out of state have been REOs, and I've been trying to figure out how to make it work here. Now I don't have to reinvent the wheel, just follow the program. You provided more information than I've ever gotten in such a short period of time. Regards and thanks,

Nell F.

I just finished Tony Alvarez's one day seminar and I have to tell you, this is one of the most valuable seminars I've ever been at. It's a lot of excellent how-to step-by-step information that you don't get from most of the other people who are teaching real estate courses. I would advise anyone who is looking for that kind of very specific information, from a guy who knows it all, to very seriously consider taking his seminar.

Rodger S.

Hey, my name is Ron Meyer and I'm a full time investor I've been doing this since 1992. I'm a hard-money lender, and real estate investor entrepreneur and I buy REO properties. I just finished attending Tony Alvarez's REO mentor class and I gotta say it was phenomenal! I learned so much. Even though I'm in the trenches doing this, there's nobody to learn more from than Tony Alvarez; He's got the resume, he's got the knowledge and if you want to learn more about this business, Tony is the guy to teach it, Tony is the guy to learn from. I really highly recommend it. Great job, Tony!

Ron Meyer

I enjoyed the diversity of subject matter.

Wendy B.

I enjoyed "GPS" as a simple business plan. I liked the breakdown of psychological vs. physical fear. I'm very excited about the positive attitude you have towards finding what does work while others are scared. I got to see specific deals, the liked the combo of humor and intensity and your desire to truly help people. You discussed being in the presence of greatness and success makers. You emphasized relationship building and what that has done for your business. You gave recommendations to follow up on pendings/short sales. Your examples of formula of an REO offer (how to get offers noticed), overcoming obstacles, "after seminar" time with Tony. Thank you for taking the time to chat with us outside of class.

Tiffany H.

There was great information and an outline of the basic steps on dealing with REO agents. Tony, it is wonderful and fun watching you give your seminar. You are an awesome teacher that not only teaches real estate but also teaches life skills, as well. Love your spirit!

Sandra P.

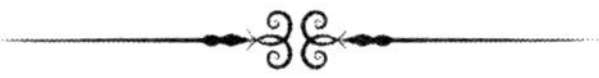

I appreciated you being straightforward.

Mark P.

I liked the fact that you were down to earth. There was no fancy "lingo." It was very informative and full of practical info.

Jane M.

Realistic numbers, real life examples, and Tony's reasons and ways to overcome fear were the best part. The info was very useful. I loved Tony's presentation and would also like to be a part of his mentorship program.

Gabriela H.

This was my first experience listening to Tony speak. I enjoyed his passionate enthusiasm and straightforward method of teaching. I live 400 miles away from Tony's home but will travel to listen to his whole seminar at a moments notice!

Ken C.

The GPS and property samples analysis were the best part of the presentation.

Albert L.

The best part was the discussion on fear and not letting it stop you from achieving your goals.

Gianfranco Z.

The thing that impresses me the most about him is where most people try to find a system that works and they sort of keep doing it, he seems to understand that that doesn't work and things only work for a certain period of time. And as fluid as the market is right now, what he seems to be doing, he's always staying ahead of the market, where's the market going next, instead of doing the same thing over and over. That's probably the biggest thing I got out of the class with him.

Nell Faulkner

I enjoyed learning about pending properties, the GPS idea and getting over your fears. Networking is so important to be around like-minded people. Tony explained many ways of getting rid of fears which is what holds up most people. It is great for people who haven't gotten started.

Rosemary D.

Very informative. It got me motivated to start looking at properties again. Knowledge is wonderful to receive and to share with others.

Jim J.

I enjoyed the action steps to position yourself for REO success in 2010.

Elvia Z.

I wanted to thank you AGAIN. I've been driving around like a madman and your interview with Carol and the special report CD really help keep me focused on the bigger picture while I'm looking at houses and appraising. The content is all straight talk and clearly comes from your heart — A welcome breather from all the Cal Worthington Real Estate crap out there. The one day is great, but the real kicker is the book and the CDs. Those items really assist me with what I need to do to get better. Thanks to you, I am growing my company and I LOVE MY OFFERS!

Peter A.

A HUGE THANK YOU for the privilege of attending your workshop last weekend in Los Angeles as a guest of yours. What an honor it was! I truly appreciate your generous spirit and caring about us, your students, by giving us the huge benefit of your knowledge, experience and expertise to "make it big" in this market.

I've been listening to your tapes this week, again, in my car from your first seminar. It pays to listen more than once because there's so much valuable information to take in.

Kathy S.

I attended your Saturday seminar and I also said "Hello" to you at Bruce's seminar. You are good! Very knowledgeable!

Gladys H.

My deepest thanks for a truly outstanding seminar last Saturday. The detailed step-by-step info and the insights into working with agents made it possibly the most valuable seminar I have taken. I look forward to seeing the internet mentoring program you are developing and possible personal participation.

Roger S.

Tony took a commonsense approach, and I could see his passion for business.

M. A.

Your ideas and expertise come from experience. You have a great attitude of success.

Tom C.

I just recently attended your seminar this past weekend. I wanted to thank you for not making it monotone and boring. It was very informative and inspiring. It is hard to find real estate investor speakers that will keep me focused for more than 10 minutes. Thank you very much, and I wish you all the luck.

Aileen N.

Very motivational; a go forth attitude!

S. W.

Tony, I ran across your website here when surfing through the web. I wanted to just let you know how much I admire you and what you have done and the advice you have given to the real estate community.

I heard you speak a couple times at different clubs and have thoroughly enjoyed listening to you speak as it has been a great inspiration. I have this one CD where you're talking with Bruce Norris about how you do what you do. I must have listened to the CD a dozen times. The one part that really stands out is when you talk about being in the people business, "and in the people business there is little or no competition." I've followed your advice 100% about caring about other people's success and developing a symbiotic relationship, and it has really started to pay off with a couple of REO agents. It's made me realize that just that little extra effort is making the difference between being average and being great.

Thanks again for your inspiration, and I hope to accomplish even half of what you have done seven years from now.

Andrew

INDEX

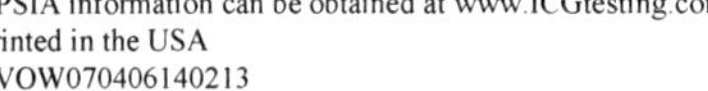

CPSIA information can be obtained at www.ICGtesting.com
Printed in the USA
LVOW070406140213

320059LV00006B/87/P

9 781453 734902